UNITY FROM ZERO TO PROFICIENCY (BEGINNER)

Second Edition

A step-by-step guide to coding your first game.

Patrick Felicia

UNITY FROM ZERO TO PROFICIENCY (BEGINNER)

First published: December 2015

Second Edition published: February 2018

Published by Patrick Felicia

Credits

Author: Patrick Felicia

About the Author

Patrick Felicia is a lecturer and researcher at Waterford Institute of Technology, where he teaches and supervises undergraduate and postgraduate students. He obtained his MSc in Multimedia Technology in 2003 and PhD in Computer Science in 2009 from University College Cork, Ireland. He has published several books and articles on the use of video games for educational purposes, including the Handbook of Research on Improving Learning and Motivation through Educational Games: Multidisciplinary Approaches (published by IGI), and Digital Games in Schools: a Handbook for Teachers, published by European Schoolnet. Patrick is also the Editor-in-chief of the International Journal of Game-Based Learning (IJGBL), and the Conference Director of the Irish Symposium on Game-Based Learning, a popular conference on games and learning organized throughout Ireland.

SUPPORT AND RESOURCES FOR THIS BOOK + FREE BOOK

As a new reader of my book series, and to thank you for choosing this book, I would like to offer you a free book. So, to receive your book, just email me at learntocreategames@gmail.com with a screenshot of your Amazon receipt and I will send you a **FREE** copy of the book "**A Quick Guide to Artificial Intelligence**" (worth **$3**), a book that will extend the content provided in this book and help you to create and include NPCs with Artificial Intelligence. After receiving your free book, you will also receive weekly updates and FREE tutorials on Unity.

>> CLAIM YOUR FREE BOOK <<

To complete the activities presented in this book you need to download the startup pack on the companion website; it consists of free resources that you will need to complete your projects, including bonus material that will help you along the way (e.g., cheat sheets, introductory videos, code samples, and much more).

These resources also include the final completed project so that you can see how your project should look like in the end.

Amongst other things, the resources for this book include:

- All the C# scripts used in this book.
- Cheat sheets with tips on how to use Unity.
- 3D characters and animation that you can use in Unity.
- A library of over 40 tutorials (video or text).

To download these resources, please do the following:

- Open the following link: http://learntocreategames.com/books/
- Select this book ("**Unity from Zero to Proficiency - Beginner**").
- On the new page, click on the link labelled "**Book Files**", or scroll down to the bottom of the page.

- In the section called "**Download your Free Resource Pack**", enter your email address and your first name, and click on the button labeled "**Yes, I want to receive my bonus pack**".
- After a few seconds, you should receive a link to your free start-up pack.

When you receive the link, you can download all the resources to your computer.

This book is dedicated to Helena & Mathis

TABLE OF CONTENTS

PREFACE

After teaching Unity for over 4 years, I always thought it could be great to find a book that could get my students started with Unity in a few hours and that showed them how to master the core functionalities offered by this fantastic software.

Many of the books that I found were too short and did not provide enough details on the why behind the actions recommended and taken; other books were highly theoretical, and I found that they lacked practicality and that they would not get my students' full attention. In addition, I often found that game development may be preferred by those with a programming background but that those with an Arts background, even if they wanted to get to know how to create games, often had to face the issue of learning to code for the first time.

As a result, I started to consider a format that would cover both: be approachable (even to the students with no programming background), keep students highly motivated and involved using an interesting project, cover the core functionalities available in Unity to get started on game programming, provide answers to common questions, and also provide, if need be, a considerable amount of details for some topics.

This book series entitled **From Zero to Proficiency** does just this. In this book series, you have the opportunity to play around with Unity's core features, and essentially those that will make it possible to create an interesting 3D game rapidly. After reading this book series, you should find it easier to use Unity and its core functionalities.

This book series assumes no prior knowledge on the part of the reader, and it will get you started on Unity so that you quickly master all the wonderful features that this software provides by going through an easy learning curve. By completing each chapter, and by following step-by-step instructions, you will progressively improve your skills, become more proficient in Unity, and create a survival game using Unity's core features in terms of programming (C# and JavaScript), game design, and drag and drop features.

In addition to understanding and being able to master Unity's core features, you will also create a game that includes many of the common techniques found in video games, including: level design, object creation, textures, collection detection, lights, weapon creation, character animations, particles, artificial intelligence, and menus.

Throughout this book series, you will create a game that includes both indoor and outdoor environments where the player needs to finds its way out of the former through tunnels, escalators, traps, and other challenges, avoid or eliminate enemies using weapons (i.e., gun or grenades), drive a car or pilot an aircraft.

You will learn how to create customized menus and simple user interfaces using Unity's new UI system, and animate and give (artificial) intelligence to Non-Player Characters (NPCs) who will be able to follow your character using Mecanim and Navmesh navigation.

Finally, you will also get to export your game for the web at the different stages of the books, so that you can share it with friends and get some feedback.

CONTENT COVERED BY THIS BOOK

Chapter 1, *Introduction to Programming in C#*, provides an introduction to C# and to core principles that will help you to get started. It explains key programming concepts such as variables, variable types, or functions.

Chapter 2, *Creating your First Script*, helps you to code your first script. It explains common coding mistakes and errors in Unity, and how to avoid them easily. It also goes through some common error messages for beginners, and explains what they mean and how they can be avoided easily.

Chapter 3, *Adding Interaction with C#*, gets you to better your scripting skills to improve your game and add more interaction. You will learn to create a scoring system, detect collisions, and to load new levels.

Chapter 4, *Creating and Updating a User Interface*, explains how you can create a user interface using Unity's UI system. You will add onscreen elements such as images, or text, and update them with your scripts to display the score and other messages to the user.

Chapter 5, *Polishing Our Game*, explains how you can improve your game, by adding a splash-screen, displaying items collected onscreen, or adding sound effects and a mini-map.

Chapter 6, Adding and Managing Simple Artificial Intelligence, introduces you to Artificial Intelligence (AI) in Unity, and explains how you can easily and simply add and manage Non-Player Characters (NPCs) that will either follow the player, or go through a simple path that you will define.

Chapter 7 provides answers to Frequently Asked Questions (FAQs) related to the topics covered in this book (e.g., scripting, audio, interaction, AI, or user interface). It also provides links to additional exclusive video tutorials that can help you with some of your questions.

Chapter 8 summarizes the topics covered in the book and provides you with more information on the next steps.

WHAT YOU NEED TO USE THIS BOOK

To complete the project presented in this book, you only need Unity 5.0, Unity 2017 (or a more recent version) and to also ensure that your computer and its operating system comply with Unity's requirements. Unity can be downloaded from the official website (**http://www.unity3d.com/download**), and before downloading, you can check that your computer is up to scratch on the following page: **http://www.unity3d.com/unity/system-requirements**. At the time of writing this book, the following operating systems are supported by Unity for development: Windows XP (i.e., SP2+, 7 SP1+), Windows 8, and Mac OS X 10.6+. In terms of graphics card, most cards produced after 2004 should be suitable.

In terms of computer skills, all knowledge introduced in this book will assume no prior programming experience from the reader. So for now, you only need to be able to perform common computer tasks, such as downloading items, opening and saving files, be comfortable with dragging and dropping items and typing, and relatively comfortable with Unity's interface. This being said, because the focus of this book is on scripting, and while all steps are explained step-by-step, you may need to be relatively comfortable with Unity's interface, as well as creating and transforming objects.

So, if you would prefer to become more comfortable with Unity prior to start scripting, you can download the first book in the series called **Unity From Zero to Proficiency (Foundations)**. This book covers most of the shortcuts and views available in Unity, as well as how to perform common tasks in Unity such as creating objects, transforming objects, importing assets, using navigation controllers, or exporting the game to the web.

WHO THIS BOOK IS FOR

If you can answer **yes** to all these questions, then this book is for you:

1. Are you a total beginner in Unity or programming?
2. Would you like to become proficient in the core functionalities offered by Unity?
3. Would you like to teach students or help your child to understand how to create games, using coding?
4. Would you like to start creating great games?
5. Although you may have had some prior exposure to Unity, would you like to delve more into Unity and understand its core functionalities in more detail?

WHO THIS BOOK IS NOT FOR

If you can answer yes to all these questions, then this book is **not** for you:

1. Can you already code with C# to implement simple behaviors such as score, collision detection, or to update the user interface.

2. Can you already easily code a 3D game with Unity with built-in objects, controllers, cameras, lights, and terrains?

3. Are you looking for a reference book on Unity programming?

4. Are you an experienced (or at least advanced) Unity user?

If you can answer yes to all four questions, you may instead look for the next books in the series. To see the content and topics covered by these books, you can check the official website (www.learntocreategames.com/books).

How you will Learn from this Book

Because all students learn differently and have different expectations of a course, this book is designed to ensure that all readers find a learning mode that suits them. Therefore, it includes the following:

- A list of the learning objectives at the start of each chapter so that readers have a snapshot of the skills that will be covered.
- Each section includes an overview of the activities covered.
- Many of the activities are step-by-step, and learners are also given the opportunity to engage in deeper learning and problem-solving skills through the challenges offered at the end of each chapter.
- Each chapter ends-up with a quiz and challenges through which you can put your skills (and knowledge acquired) into practice, and see how much you know. Challenges consist in coding, debugging, or creating new features based on the knowledge that you have acquired in the chapter.
- The book focuses on the core skills that you need; some sections also go into more detail; however, once concepts have been explained, links are provided to additional resources, where necessary.
- The code is introduced progressively and is explained in detail.

Format of Each Chapter and Writing Conventions

Throughout this book, and to make reading and learning easier, text formatting and icons will be used to highlight parts of the information provided and to make it more readable.

The full solution for the project presented in this book is available for download on the official website (http://learntocreategames.com/books). So if you need to skip a section, you can do so; you can also download the solution for the previous chapter that you have skipped.

Special Notes

Each chapter includes resource sections so that you can further your understanding and mastery of Unity; these include:

- A quiz for each chapter: these quizzes usually include 10 questions that test your knowledge of the topics covered throughout the chapter. The solutions are provided on the companion website.
- A checklist: it consists of between 5 and 10 key concepts and skills that you need to be comfortable with before progressing to the next chapter.
- Challenges: each chapter includes a challenge section where you are asked to combine your skills to solve a particular problem.

Author's notes appear as described below:

> Author's suggestions appear in this box.

Code appears as described below:

```
int score;
string playersName = "Sam";
```

Checklists that include the important points covered in the chapter appear as described below:

- Item1 for check list
- Item2 for check list
- Item3 for check list

HOW CAN YOU LEARN BEST FROM THIS BOOK?

- **Talk to your friends about what you are doing.**

  We often think that we understand a topic until we have to explain it to friends and answer their questions. By explaining your different projects, what you just learned will become clearer to you.

- **Do the exercises.**

  All chapters include exercises that will help you to learn by doing. In other words, by completing these exercises, you will be able to better understand the topic and gain practical skills (i.e., rather than just reading).

- **Don't be afraid of making mistakes.**

  I usually tell my students that making mistakes is part of the learning process; the more mistakes you make and the more opportunities you have for learning. At the start, you may find the errors disconcerting, or that the engine does not work as expected until you understand what went wrong.

- **Export your games early.**

  It is always great to build and export your first game. Even if it is rather simple, it is always good to see it in a browser and to be able to share it with you friends.

- **Learn in chunks.**

  It may be disconcerting to go through five or six chapters straight, as it may lower your motivation. Instead, give yourself enough time to learn, go at your own pace, and learn in small units (e.g., between 15 and 20 minutes per day). This will do at least two things for you: it will give your brain the time to "digest" the information that you have just learned, so that you can start fresh the following day. It will also make sure that you don't "burn-out" and that you keep your motivation levels high.

FEEDBACK

While I have done everything possible to produce a book of high quality and value, I always appreciate feedback from readers so that the book can be improved accordingly. If you would like to give feedback, you can email me at learntocreategames@gmail.com.

DOWNLOADING THE SOLUTIONS FOR THE BOOK

You can download the solutions for this book after creating a free online account at http://learntocreategames.com/books/. Once you have registered, a link to the files will be sent to you automatically.

IMPROVING THE BOOK

Although great care was taken in checking the content of this book, I am human, and some errors could remain in the book. As a result, it would be great if you could let me know of any issue or error you may have come across in this book, so that it can be solved and the book updated accordingly. To report an error, you can email me (learntocreategames@gmail.com) with the following information:

- Name of the book.
- The page where the error was detected.
- Describe the error and also what you think the correction should be.

Once your email is received, the error will be checked, and, in the case of a valid error, it will be corrected and the book page will be updated to reflect the changes accordingly.

SUPPORTING THE AUTHOR

A lot of work has gone into this book and it is the fruit of long hours of preparation, brainstorming, and finally writing. As a result, I would ask that you do not distribute any illegal copies of this book.

This means that if a friend wants a copy of this book, s/he will have to buy it through the official channels (i.e., through Amazon, lulu.com, or the book's official website: http://www.learntocreategames.com/books).

If some of your friends are interested in the book, you can refer them to the book's official website (http://www.learntocreategames.com/books) where they can either buy the book, enter a monthly draw to be in for a chance of receiving a free copy of the book, or to be notified of future promotional offers.

1

INTRODUCTION TO PROGRAMMING IN C#

In this section we will discover C# programming principles and concepts, so that you can start programming in the next chapter. If you have already coded using C# (or a similar language), you can skip this chapter.

After completing this chapter, you will be able to:

- Understand key differences between UnityScript and C#.
- Understand the reasons why you need to consider C#.
- Understand object-oriented programming (OOP) concepts when coding in C#.
- Get used to and understand the concepts of variables, methods, and scope.
- Understand key best practices for coding, particularly in C#.
- Understand conditional statements and decision making structures.
- Understand the concept of loops.

WHY USE C# INSTEAD OF JAVASCRIPT

From 2017 onwards, UnityScript is no longer supported in Unity; so while the first version of this book was using JavaScript, this new and updated version is focusing in C# instead. By learning C# within Unity, you get to discover a new language that is object-oriented, relatively easy to learn, and with strong resemblances with Java (another widespread object-oriented language. Another advantage of using C# is that it may be a good asset if you would like to pursue a career in the gaming industry, as many gaming companies use this language.

INTRODUCTION

When scripting in Unity, you are communicating with the Game Engine and asking it to perform actions. To communicate with the system, you are using a language or a set of words bound by a syntax that the computer and you know. This language consists of keywords, key phrases, and a syntax that ensures that the instructions are understood properly. In computer science, this sentence needs to be exact, precise, unambiguous, and with a correct syntax. In other words, it needs to be **exact**. The syntax is a set of rules that are followed when writing code in C# (as for JavaScript). In addition to its syntax, C# programming also uses classes; so your scripts will be saved as classes.

In the next section, we will learn how to use this syntax. If you have already coded in JavaScript, some of the information provided in the rest of this chapter may look familiar and this prior exposure to JavaScript will definitely help you. This being said, UnityScript and C#, despite some relative similarities, are quite different in many aspects (e.g., variable declaration, function declaration, etc.).

When scripting in C#, you will be using a combination of the following:

- Classes.
- Objects.
- Statements.
- Comments.
- Variables.
- Constants.
- Operators.
- Assignments.
- Data types.
- Methods.
- Decision making structures.
- Loops.
- Inheritance (more advanced).
- Polymorphism (more advanced).
- Operator overloading (more advanced).

- Interfaces.
- Name spaces.
- Events.
- Comparisons.
- Type conversions.
- Reserved words.
- Messages to the console windows.
- Declarations.
- Calls to methods.

The list may look a bit intimidating but, not to worry, we will explore these in the next sections, and you will get to know and use them smoothly using hands-on examples.

STATEMENTS

When you write a piece of C# code, you need to tell the system to execute your instructions (e.g., print information) using statements. A statement is literally an order or something you ask the system to do. For example, in the next line of code, the statement will tell Unity to print a message in the **Console** window:

```
print ("Hello Word");
```

When writing statements, there are a few rules that you need to know:

- Order of statements: each statement is executed in the order it appears in the script. For example, in the next example, the code will print **hello**, then **world;** this is because the associated statements are in that particular sequence.

```
print ("hello");
print ("world");
```

- Statements are separated by **semi-colons** (i.e., semi-colon at the end of each statement).

Note that several statements can be added on the same line, as long as they are separated by a semi-colon.

- For example the next line of code has a correct syntax.

```
print("hello");print ("world");
```

- Multiple spaces are ignored for statements; however, it is good practice to add spaces around the operators such as +, -, /, or **%** for clarity. For example, in the next example, we say that **a** is equal to **b**. There is a space both before and after the operator =.

```
a = b;
```

- Statements to be executed together (e.g., based on the same condition) can be grouped using what is usually referred to as **code blocks**. In C# (as for JavaScript), code blocks are symbolized by curly brackets (e.g., { or }). So, in other words, if you needed to group several statements, we would include them all within the same curly brackets, as follows:

```
{
        print ("hello stranger!");
        print ("today, we will learn about scripting");
}
```

As we have seen earlier, a statement usually employs or starts with a keyword (i.e., a word that the computer knows). Each of these keywords has a specific purpose and the most common ones (at this stage) are used for:

- Printing a message in the **Console** window: the keyword is **print**.
- Declaring a variable: the keyword depends on the type of variable (e.g., **int** for integers, **string** for text, **bool** for Boolean variables, etc.) and we will see more about this in the next sections.
- Declaring a method: the keyword depends on the type of the data returned by the method. For example, in C#, the name of a method is preceded by the keyword **int** when the method returns an **integer**, **string** when the method returns a **string**, or **void** when the method does not return any information.

What is called a **method** in C# is what used to be called a function in UnityScript; these terms (i.e., function and method) differ in at least two ways: in C# you need to specify the type of the data returned by this method, and the keyword **function** is not used anymore in C# for this purpose. We will see more about this topic in the next sections.

- Marking a block of instructions to be executed based on a condition: the keywords are **if…else**.
- Exiting a function: the keyword is **return**.

Comments

In C# (similarly to JavaScript), you can use comments to explain the code and to make it more readable. This becomes important as the size of your code increases; and it is also important if you work as part of a team, so that team members can understand your code and make amendments in the right places, if and when it is needed.

When code is commented, it is not executed. There are two ways to comment your code in C#; you can use **single** or **multi-line** comments. In single-line comments, a **double forward slash** is added at the start of a line or after a statement, so that this line (or part thereof) is commented, as illustrated in the next code snippet.

```
//the next line prints Hello in the console window
print ("Hello");
//the next line declares the variable name
string name;
name = "Hello";//sets the value of the variable name
```

In multi-line comments, any text between /* and */ will be commented (and not executed). This is also refereed as **comment blocks**.

```
/* the next lines after the comments print hello in the console window
we then declare the variable name and assign a value
*/
print("Hello");
string name;
name = "Hello";//sets the value of the variable name
//print ("Hello World")
/*
       string name;
       name = "My Name";

*/
```

In addition to providing explanations about your code, you can also use comments to prevent part of your code to be executed. This is very useful when you would like to debug your code and find where the error or bug might be, using a very simple method. By commenting sections of your code, and using a process of elimination, you can usually find the issue quickly. For example, you can comment all the code and run the script; then comment half the code, and run the script. If it works, it means that the error is within the code that has been commented, and if it does not work, it means that the error is in the code that has not been commented. In the first case (if the code works), we could then just comment half of the portion of the code that has already been commented. So, by successively commenting more specific areas of our code, we can get to discover what part of the code includes the bug. This process is often called **dichotomy** (as we successively divide a code section into two). It is usually effective to debug your code because the number of iterations (dividing part of the code in two) is more predictable and also potentially less time-consuming. For example, for 100 lines of codes, we can successively narrow down the issue to 50, 25, 12, 6, and 3 lines (5 to 6 iterations in this case would be necessary instead of going through the whole 100 lines).

Variables

A variable is a container. It includes a value that may change overtime. When using variables, we usually need to: (1) declare the variable (by specifying its type), (2) assign a value to this variable, and (3) possibly combine this variable with other variables using operators.

```
int myAge;//we declare the variable
myAge = 20;// we set the variable to 20
myAge = myAge + 1; //we add 1 to the variable myAge
```

In the previous example, we have declared a variable **myAge**, its type is **int** (integer), we set it to **20** and we then add 1 to it.

> Note that, contrary to UnityScript where the keyword **var** is used to declare a variable, in C# the variable is declared using its type followed by its name. As we will see later we will also need to use what is called an **access modifier** in order to specify how this variable can be accessed.

> Note that in the previous code we have assigned the value **myAge + 1** to **myAge**; the = operator is an assignment operator; in other words, it is there to assign a value to a variable and is not to be understood in a strict algebraic sense (i.e., that the values or variables on both sides of the = sign are equal).

Contrary to UnityScript, and to make coding easier and leaner, in C# you can perform a multiple declaration of several variables of the same type in the same statement. For example, in the next code snippet, we declare three variables, **v1**, **v2**, and **v3** in one statement. This is because they are of the same type (i.e., **integers**).

```
int v1,v2,v3;
int v4=4, v5=5, v6=6;
```

In the code above, the first line declares the variables v1, v2, and v3. All three are integers. In the second line, not only do we declare three variables simultaneously, but we also initialize them (i.e., set a value).

When using variables, there are a few things that we need to determine including their name, type and scope:

- **Name of a variable:** A variable is usually given a unique name so that it can be identified uniquely. The name of a variable is usually referred to as an identifier. When defining an identifier, it can contain letters, digits, a minus, an underscore or a dollar sign, and it usually begins with a letter. Identifiers cannot be keywords (e.g., such as **if**).

- **Type of variable:** variables can hold several types of data including numbers (e.g., **integers, doubles** or **floats**), text (i.e., strings or characters), Boolean values (e.g., true or false), arrays, objects (i.e., we will see this concept later in this chapter) or **GameObjects** (i.e., any object included in your scene), as illustrated in the next code snippet.

```
string myName = "Patrick";//the text is declared using double quotes
int currentYear = 2015;//the year needs no decimals and is declared as an integer
float width = 100.45f;//width is declared as a float (i.e., with decimals)
```

- **Variable declaration:** a variable needs to be declared so that the system knows what you referring to if you use it in your code. To create a variable, it needs to be declared. At the declaration stage, the variable does not have to be assigned a value, and this can be done later.

```
string myName;
myName = "My Name"
```

In the previous example, we declare a variable called **myName** and then assign the value **"My Name"** to it.

- **Scope of a variable:** a variable can be accessed (i.e., referred to) in specific contexts that depend on where in the script the variable was declared. We will look at this principle later.

- **Accessibility level:** as we will see later, a C# programme consists of classes; for each of these classes, the methods and variables within can be accessed depending on **accessibility** levels. We will look at this principle later on (there is no need for any confusion at this stage :-)).

Common variable types include:

- **String**: same as text.

- **Int**: integer (1, 2, 3, etc.).

- **Boolean**: true or false.

- **Float**: with a fractional value (e.g., 1.2f, 3.4f, etc.).

- **Arrays**: a group of variables of the same type. If this is unclear, not to worry, this concept will be explained further in this chapter.

- **GameObject**: a game object (any game object in your scene).

ARRAYS

Sometimes, to make your code leaner, arrays make it easier to apply features and similar behaviors to a wide range of data. Arrays can help to declare less variables (for variables storing the same type of information) and to also access them more easily. When creating arrays, you can create single-dimensional arrays and multidimensional arrays.

Let's look at the simplest form of arrays: single-dimensional arrays. For this concept, we can take the analogy of a group of 10 people who all have a name. If we wanted to store this information using a string variable, we would need to declare (and set) ten different variables.

```
string name1;string name2; ......
```

While this code is perfectly fine, it would be great to store these in only one variable. For this purpose, we could use an array. An array is comparable to a list of elements that we access using an index. This index usually starts at 0 (for the first element in the list).

So let's see how we could do this with an array; first we could declare the array as follows:

```
string [] names;
```

You will probably notice the syntax **dataType [] nameofTheArray**. The **[]** syntax means that we declare an **array** of string values.

Then we could initialize the array, as we would normally do with any variable:

```
names = new string [10];
```

In the previous code, we just say that our new array called **names** will include 10 string variables.

We can then store information in this array as described in the next code snippet.

```
names [0] = "Paul";
names [1] = "Mary";
...
names [9] = "Pat";
```

In the previous code, we store the name **Paul** as the first element in the array (remember the index starts at 0); we store the second element (with the index 1) as **Mary**, as well as the last element (index is 9), **Pat**.

Note that for an array of size **n**, **the index of the first element is 0** and **the index of the last element is n-1**. So for an array of size 10, the index for the first element is 0, and the index of the last element is 9.

If you were to use arrays of integers or floats, or any other type of data, the process would be similar.

Now, one of the cool things you can do with arrays is that you can initialize your array in one line, saving you the headaches of writing 10 lines of code if you have 10 variables, as illustrated in the next example.

```
string [] names = new string [10] {"Paul","Mary","John","Mark",
"Eva","Pat","Sinead","Elma","Flaithri", "Eleanor"};
```

This is very handy, as you will see in the next chapters, and this should definitely save you time coding.

Now that we have looked into single-dimensional arrays, let's look at multidimensional arrays, which can also be very handy when storing information. This type of array (i.e., multidimensional array) can be compared to a building with several floors, and on each floor, several apartments. So let's say that we would like to store the number of tenants for each apartment; we would, in this case, create variables that would store this number for each of these apartments.

The first solution would be to create variables that store the number of tenants for each of these apartments with a variable that makes reference to the floor, and the number of the apartment. For example **ap0_1** could be for the first apartment on the ground floor, **ap0_2**, would then be for the second apartment on the ground floor, **ap1_1**, would then be for the first apartment on the first floor, and **ap1_2**, would then be for the second apartment on the first floor. So in term of coding, we could have the following:

```
int ap0_1 = 0;
int ap0_2 = 0;
...
```

Using arrays instead we could do the following:

```
int [,] apArray = new int [10,10];
apArray [0,1] = 0;
apArray [0,2] = 0;
print (apArray[0]);
```

In the previous code:

- We declare our array. **int [,]** means an array that has two dimensions; in other words, we say that any element in this array will be defined and accessed based on two parameters: the floor level and the number of this apartment on that level.

- We also specify a size (or maximum) for each of these parameters. The maximum number of floors (level) will be 10, and the maximum number of apartment per floor will be 10. So, for this example we can define levels, from level 0 to level 9 (that would be 10 levels), and from apartment 0 to apartment 9 (that would be 10 apartment).

- The last line of code prints (in the **Console** window) the value of the first element of the array.

One of the other interesting things with arrays is that, using a loop, you can write a single line of code to access all the elements of this array, and hence, write more efficient code.

CONSTANTS

So far we have looked at variables and how you can store and access them seamlessly. The assumption then was that a value may change over time, and that this value would be stored in a variable. However, there may be times when you know that a value will remain constant. For example, you may want to define labels that refer to values that should not change over time, and in this case, you could use constants. Let me explain: let's say that the player may have three choices in the game (e.g., referred to as 0, 1, and 2) and that you don't really want to remember these values, or that you would like to use a way that makes it easier to refer to them. Let's look at the following code:

```
int userChoice = 2;
if (userChoice == 0) print ("you have decided to restart");
if (userChoice == 1) print ("you have decided to stop the game");
if (userChoice == 2) print ("you have decided to pause the game");
```

In the previous code:

- The variable **userChoice** is an integer and is set to 1.
- Then we check its value and print a message accordingly.

Now, you may or may not remember that 0 corresponds to restarting the game; the same applies to the other two values. So instead, we could use constants to make it easier to remember (and use) these values. Let's look at the equivalent code that uses constants.

```
const int CHOICE_RESTART = 0;
const int CHOICE_STOP = 1;
const int CHOICE_PAUSE = 2;
int userChoice = 2;
if (userChoice == CHOICE_RESTART) print ("you have decided to restart");
if (userChoice == CHOICE_STOP) print ("you have decided to stop the game");
if (userChoice == CHOICE_PAUSE) print ("you have decided to pause the game");
```

In the previous code:

- We declare three **constant** variables.
- These variables are then used to check the choice made by the user.

In the next example, we use a constant to calculate a tax rate; this is a good practice as the same value will be used across the programme with no or little room for errors when it comes to using the exact same tax rate across the code.

```
const float VAT_RATE = 0.21f;
float priceBeforeVat = 23.0f
float priceAfterVat = pricebeforeVat * VAT_RATE;
```

In the previous code:

- We declare a **constant** float variable for the vat rate.
- We declare a **float** variable for the item's price before the vat.
- We calculate the item's price after adding tax.

It is a very good coding practice to use constants for values that don't change across your programmme. Using constants makes your code more readable; it saves work when you need to change a value in your code, and it also decreases possible occurrences of errors (e.g., for calculations).

OPERATORS

Once we have declared and assigned values to a variable, we can use operators to modify or combine variables. There are different types of operators including: arithmetic operators, assignment operators, comparison operators and logical operators.

Arithmetic operators are used to perform arithmetic operations including additions, subtractions, multiplications, or divisions. Common arithmetic operators include +, -, *, /, or **%** (modulo).

```
int number1 = 1;// the variable number1 is declared
int number2 = 1;// the variable number2 is declared
int sum = number1 + number2;// adding two numbers and store them in sum
int sub = number1 - number2;// subtracting two numbers and store them in sub
```

Assignment operators can be used to assign a value to a variable and include =, +=, -=, *=, /= or %=.

```
int number1 = 1;
int number2 = 1;
number1+=1; //same as number1 = number1 + 1;
number1-=1; //same as number1 = number1 - 1;
number1*=1; //same as number1 = number1 * 1;
number1/=1; //same as number1 = number1 / 1;
number1%=1; //same as number1 = number1 % 1;
```

Note that the = operator, when used with strings, will concatenate strings (i.e., add them one after the other to create a new string). When used with a number and a string, the same will apply (for example **"Hello"+1** will result in "**Hello1**").

Comparison operators are often used for conditions to compare two values; comparison operators include ==, !=, >, <, >= and >=.

```
if (number1 == number2); //if number1 equals number2
if (number1 != number2); //if number1 and number2 have different values
if (number1 > number2); //if number1 is greater than number2
if (number1 >= number2); //if number1 is greater than or equal to number2
if (number1 < number2); //if number1 is less than number2
if (number1 <= number2); //if number1 is less than or equal to number2
```

CONDITIONAL STATEMENTS

Statements can be performed based on a condition, and in this case they are called **conditional statements**. The syntax is usually as follows:

```
If (condition) statement;
```

This means **if the condition is verified (or true) then (and only then) the statement is executed**. When we assess a condition, we test whether a declaration is true. For example by typing **if (a == b)**, we mean **"if it is true that a equals to b"**. Similarly, if we type **if (a>=b)** we mean **"if its is true that a is greater than or equal to b"**

As we will see later on, we can also combine conditions. For example, we can decide to perform a statement if two (or more) conditions are true. For example, by typing **if (a == b && c == 2)** we mean **"if a equals to b and c equals to 2"**. In this case using the operator **&&** means **AND**, and that both conditions will need to be true. We could compare this to making a decision on whether we will go sailing tomorrow. For example "**if the weather is sunny and the wind speed is less than 5km/h then I will go sailing**". We could translate this statement as follows.

```
if (weatherIsSunny == true && windSpeed < 5) IGoSailing = true;
```

When creating conditions, as for most natural languages, we can use the operator **OR** noted **||**. Taking the previous example, we could translate the following sentence "**if the weather is too hot or the wind is faster than 5km/h then I will not go sailing** " as follows.

```
if (weatherIsTooHot == true || windSpeed >5) IGoSailing = false;
```

Another example could be as follows.

```
if (myName == "Patrick") print("Hello Patrick");
else print ("Hello Stranger");
```

When we deal with combining true or false statements, we are effectively applying what is called **Boolean logic**. Boolean logic deals with Boolean variables that have two values 1 and 0 (or true and false). By evaluating conditions, we are effectively processing Boolean numbers and applying Boolean logic. While you don't need to know about Boolean logic in depth, some operators for Boolean logic are important, including the **!** operator. It means **NOT** or the opposite. This means that if a variable is true, its opposite will be false, and vice versa. For example, if we consider the variable **weatherIsGood = true**, the value of **!weatherIsGood** will be **false** (its opposite). So the condition **if (weatherIdGood == false)** could be also written **if (!weatherIsGood)** which would literally translate as "if the weather is **NOT** good".

SWITCH STATEMENTS

If you have understood the concept of conditional statements, then this section should be pretty much straight forward. Switch statements are a variation on the if/else statements that we have seen earlier. The idea behind the switch statement is that, depending on the value of a particular variable, we will switch to a particular portion of the code and perform one or several actions. The variable considered for the switch structure is usually of type **integer**. Let's look at a simple example:

```
int choice = 1;
switch (choice)
{
        case 1:
                print ("you chose 1");
                break;
        case 2:
                print ("you chose 2");
                break;
        case 3:
                print ("you chose 3");
                break;
        default:
                print ("Default option");
                break;
}
print ("We have exited the switch structure");
```

In the previous code:

- We declare the variable **choice**, as an **integer** and initialize it to **1**.
- We then create a **switch** structure whereby, depending on the value of the variable **choice**, the programme will switch to the relevant section (i.e., the portion of code starting with **case 1:**, **case 2:**, etc.). Note that in our code, we look for the values 1, 2 or 3. However, if the variable **choice** does not equal 1 or 2 or 3, the program will branch to the section called **default**. This is because this section is executed if any of the other possible choices (i.e., 1,2, or 3) have not been fulfilled (or selected).

Note that each choice or branch starts with the keyword **case** and ends with **break**. The **break** statement is there to specify that after executing the commands included in the branch (or current choice), it should exit the switch structure. Without any break statement the next line of code will be executed.

So let's consider the previous example and see how this would work. In our case, the variable **choice** is set to **1**, so we will enter the **switch** structure, and then look for the section that deals with a value of **1** for the variable **choice**. This will be the section that starts with **case 1:**; then the command **print ("you chose 1");** will be executed, followed by the command **break**, indicating that we should exit the switch structure; finally the command **print ("We have exited the switch structure")** will be executed.

Switch structures are very useful to structure your code and when dealing with mutually exclusive choices (i.e., only one of the choices can be processed) based on an integer value, especially in the case of menus. In addition, switch structures make for cleaner and easily understandable code.

LOOPS

There are times when you have to perform repetitive tasks as a programmer; many times, these can be fast forwarded using loops. Loops are structures that will perform the same actions repetitively based on a condition. So, the process is usually as follows:

- Start the loop.
- Perform actions.
- Check for a condition.
- Exit the loop if the condition is fulfilled or keep looping.

Sometimes the condition is performed at the start of the loop, some other times it is performed at the end of the loop.

Let's take the following example that is using a **while** loop.

```
int counter =0;
while (counter <=10)
{
      print ("Counter = " + counter);
      counter++;
}
```

In the previous code:

- We set the value of the variable **counter**.
- We then create a loop that is delimited by the curly brackets and that starts with the keyword **while**.
- We set the condition to remain in this loop (i.e., **counter <=10**).
- Within the loop, we increase the value of the variable **counter** by 1 and print its value.

So effectively:

- The first time we go through the loop: the variable **counter** is increased to **1**; we reach the end of the loop; we go back to the start of the loop and check if **counter** is <=10; this is true in this case (**counter** = 1).
- The second time we go through the loop: **counter** is increased to 2; we reach the end of the loop; we go back to the start of the loop and check if **counter** is <=10; this is true in this case (**counter** = **2**).

- ...
- The 11th time we go through the loop: **counter** is increased to 11; we reach the end of the loop; we go back to the start and check if **counter** is <=10; this is now false in this case (**counter** = 11). As a result, we then exit the loop.

So, as you can see, using a loop, we have managed to increment the value of the variable **counter** iteratively, from 0 to 11, but using less code than would be needed otherwise.

Now, we could create a slightly modified version of this loop; let's look at the following example:

```
int counter =0;
do
{
	print ("Counter = " + counter);
	counter++;
} while (counter <=10);
```

In this example, you may spot two differences, compared to the previous code:

- The **while** keyword is now at the end of the loop. So the condition will be evaluated (or assessed) at the end of the loop.
- A **do** keyword is now featured at the start of the loop.
- In this example, we perform statements and then check for the condition.

Another variations of the code could be as follows:

```
for (int counter = 0; counter <=10; counter ++)
{
	print ("Counter = " + counter);
}
```

In the previous code:

- We declare a loop in a slight different way: we say that we will use an integer variable called **counter** that will go from 0 to 10.
- This variable **counter** will be incremented by 1 every time we go through the loop.
- We remain in the loop as long as the variable **counter** is less than or equal to 10.
- The test for the condition, in this case, is performed at the start of the loop.

Loops are very useful to be able to perform repetitive actions for a finite number of objects, or to perform what is usually referred as recursive actions. For example, you could use loops to create (i.e., instantiate) 100 objects at different locations (this will save you some code :-)), or to go through an array of 100+ elements.

CLASSES

When coding in C# with Unity, you will be creating scripts that are either classes or use built-in classes. So what is a class?

As we have seen earlier, C# is an object-Oriented programming (OOP) language. Put simply, a C# programme will consist of a collection of objects that interact amongst themselves. Each object has one or more attributes, and it is possible to perform actions on these objects using what are called **methods**. In addition, objects that share the same properties are said to belong to the same **class**. For example, we could take the analogy of a bike. There are bikes of all shapes and colors; however, they share common features. For example, they all have a specific number of wheels (e.g., one, two or three) or a speed; they can have a color, and actions can be performed on these bikes (e.g., accelerate, turn right, turn left, etc.). So in object-oriented programming, the class would be **bike**, speed or color would be referred as member variables, and accelerate (i.e., an action) would be referred as member methods. So if we were to define a common type, we could define a class called **Bike** and for this class define several member variables and attributes that would make it possible to define and perform actions on the objects of type **Bike**.

This is, obviously, a simplified explanation of classes and objects, but it should give you a clearer idea of the concept of object-oriented programming, if you are new to it.

DEFINING A CLASS

So now that we have a clearer idea of what a class is, let's see how we could define a class. So let's look at the following example.

```
public class Bike
{
	private float speed;
	private int color;

	private void accelerate()
	{
		speed++;
	}
	private void turnRight()
	{
	}

}
```

In the code above, we have defined a class, called **Bike**, that includes two member variables (**speed** and **color**) as well as two member methods (**accelerate** and **turnRight**). Let's look at the script a little closer; you may notice a few things:

- The name of the class is preceded by the keywords **public class**; in OOP terms, the keyword **public** is called an **access modifier** and it defines how (and from where) this class may be accessed and used. In C# there are at least five types of access modifiers, including **public** (no restricted access), **protected** (access limited to the containing class or types derived from this class), **internal** (access is limited to the current assembly), **protected internal** (we won't be using this access mode in this book), and **private** (access only from the containing type).

- The names of all variables are preceded by their type (i.e., int), and the keyword **private**: this means that these integer variables will be accessible only for objects of types **Bike**.

- The name of each method is preceded by the keywords **private void**: the **void** keyword means that the method does not return any data back, while the keyword **private** means that the method will be accessible only from the containing type (i.e., **Bike**). In other word, only objects of type **Bike** will be able to access this method.

ACCESSING CLASS MEMBERS AND VARIABLES

Once a class has been defined, it's great to be able to access its member variables and methods. In C# (as for other object-oriented programming languages), this can be done using the **dot notation**.

> The dot notation refers to **object-oriented programming**. Using dots, you can access properties and functions (or methods) related to a particular object. For example **gameObject.transform.position** gives you access to the **position** from the **transform** of the object linked to this script. It is often useful to read it backward; in this case, the dot can be interpreted as **"of"**. So in our case, **gameObject.transform.position** can be translated as "the position **of** the transform **of** the **gameObject**".

Once a class has been defined, objects based on this class can be created. For example, if we were to create a new **Bike** object, based on the code that we have seen above, the following code could be used.

```
Bike myBike = new Bike();
```

This code will create an object based on the "template" **Bike**. You may notice the syntax:

```
dataType variable = new dataType()
```

By default, this new object will include all the member variables and methods defined earlier. So it will have a color and a speed, and we should also be able to access its **accelerate** and **turnRight** methods. So how can this be done? Let's look at the next code snippet that shows how we can access these.

```
Bike b = new Bike();
b.speed = 12.3f
b.color = 2;
b.accelerate();
```

In the previous code:

- The new bike **myBike** is created.
- Its speed is set to **12.3** and its color to **2**.
- The speed is then increased after calling the **accelerate** method.
- Note that to assign an object's attribute or method we use the dot notation.

When defining member variables and methods, it is usually good practice to restrict the access to member variables (e.g., private type) and to define public methods with no or less strict restrictions (e.g., public) that provide access to these variables. These methods are often referred to as **getters** and **setters** (because you can get or set values from them).

To illustrate this concept, let's look at the following code:

```
public class Bike
{
        private float speed;
        private int color;

        private void accelerate()
        {
                speed++;
        }
        public void setSpeed (float newSpeed)
        {
                speed = newSpeed;
        }
        public float getSpeed ()
        {
                return (speed)
        }

        private void turnRight()
        {
        }

}
```

In the previous code, we have declared two new methods: **setSpeed** and **getSpeed**.

- For **setSpeed**: the type is **void** as this method does not return any information, and its access is set to **public**, so that it can be accessed with no restrictions.
- For **getSpeed**: the type is **float** as this method returns the speed, which type is float. Its access is set to **public**, so that it can be accessed with no restrictions.

So, we could combine the code created to date in one programme (or new class) as follows in Unity.

```
using UnityEngine;
using System.Collections;

public class TestCode : MonoBehaviour {
      public class Bike
      {
            private float speed;
            private int color;

            private void accelerate()
            {
                  speed++;
            }
            public void setSpeed (float newSpeed)
            {
                  speed = newSpeed;
            }
            public float getSpeed ()
            {
                  return (speed);
            }

            private void turnRight()
            {
            }
      }
      public void Start ()
      {
            Bike myBike = new Bike();
            myBike.setSpeed (23.0f);
            print (myBike.getSpeed());
      }
}
```

In the previous code, you may notice at least two differences compared to the previous code that we have created:

- At the start of the code, the following two lines of code have been added:

```
using UnityEngine;
using System.Collections;
```

- The keyword **using** is called a directive; in this particular case it is used to import what is called a **namespace**; put simply, by adding this directive you are effectively importing (or gaining access to) a collection of classes or data types. Each of these namespaces or "libraries" includes useful classes for your programme. For example the namespace **UnityEngine** will include classes for Unity development and **System.Collections** will include classes and interfaces for different collections of objects. By default, whenever you create a new C# script in Unity, these two namespaces (and associated directives) are included.

- We have declared our class **Bike** within another class called **TestCode**. **TestCode** is, in this case, the containing class.

```
public class TestCode : MonoBehaviour {
```

- Whenever you create a new C# script, the name of the script (for example **TestCode** will be used to define the main class within the script; i.e., **TestCode**).

- The **syntax : Monobehavior** means that the class **TestCode** is derived from the class **MonoBehaviour**. This is often referred to as inheritance.

CONSTRUCTORS

As we have seen in the previous section, when a new object is created, it will, by default, include all the member variables and methods. To create this object, we would use the name of the class, followed by **()**, as per the next example.

```
Bike myBike = new Bike();
myBike.color = 2;
myBike.speed = 12.3f;
```

In fact, it is possible to change some of the properties of the new object created at the time it is initialized. For example, instead of setting the speed and the color of the object as we have done in the previous code, it would be great to be able to set these automatically and pass the parameter accordingly when the object is created. Well, this can be done with what is called a **constructor**. A constructor literally helps to construct your new object based on parameters (also referred as arguments) and instructions. So, for example, let's say that we would like the color of our bike to be specified when it is created; we could modify the **Bike** class, as follows, by adding the following method:

```
public Bike (int newColor)
{
	color = newColor;
}
```

This is a new constructor (the name of the method is the same as the class), and it takes an integer as a parameter; so after modifying the description of our class (as per the code above), we could then create a new bike object as follows:

```
Bike myBike = new Bike(2);
//myBike.color = 2;
myBike.speed = 12.3f;
```

We could even specify a second constructor that would include both the color and the speed as follows:

```
public Bike (int newColor, float newSpeed)
{
	color = newColor;
	speed = newSpeed;
}
```

You can have different constructors in your class; the constructor used at the initialization stage will be the one that matches the arguments passed.

For example, let's say that we have two constructors for our Bike class.

```
public Bike (int newColor, float newSpeed)
{
        color = newColor;
        speed = newSpeed;
}
public Bike (int newColor)
{
        color = newColor;
}
```

If a new **Bike** object is created as follows:

```
Bike newBike = new Bike (2)
```

...then the first constructor will be called.

If a new **Bike** object is created as follows:

```
Bike newBike = new Bike (2, 10.0f)
```

...then the second constructor will be called.

You may also wonder what happens if the following code is used since no default constructor has been defined.

```
Bike newBike = new Bike ();
```

In fact, whenever you create your class, a default constructor is also defined (implicitly) and evoked whenever a new object is created using the **new** operator with no arguments. This is called a default constructor. In this case, the default values for each of the types of the numerical member variables are used (e.g., 0 for integers or false for Boolean variables).

> Note that access to constructors is usually public, except in the particular cases where we would like a class not to be instantiated (e.g., for classes that include **static** members only). Also note that, as for variables, if no access modifiers are specified, these will be **private** by default. This is similar for methods.

Destructors

As for constructors, when an object is deleted, the corresponding destructor is called. Its name is the same as the class and preceded by a tilde ~; as illustrated in the next code snippet.

```
~Bike()
{
      print("Object has been destroyed");
}
```

This being said, a destructor can neither take parameters (or arguments) nor return a value.

STATIC MEMBERS OF A CLASS

When a method or variable is declared as static, only one instance of this member exists for a class. So a static variable will be "shared" between instances of this class. Static variables are usually used to retrieve constants without instantiating a class. The same applies for static method: they can be evoked without having to instantiate a class. This can be very useful if you want to create and avail of tools. For example, in Unity, it is possible to use the method **GameObject.Find**(); this method usually makes it possible to look for a particular object based on its name. Let's look at the following example.

```
public void  Start()
{
      GameObject t = (GameObject) GameObject.Find("test");
}
```

In the previous code, we look for an object called test, and store the result inside the variable **t** of type **GameObject**. However, when we use the syntax **GameObject.Find**, we use the static method **Find** that is available from the class **GameObject**. There are many other static functions that you will be able to use in Unity, including **Instantiate**. Again, these functions can be called without the need to instantiate an object. The following code snippet provides another example based on the class **Bike**.

```
using UnityEngine;
using System.Collections;

public class TestCode : MonoBehaviour {

	public class Bike
	{
		private float speed;
		private int color;
		private static nbBikes;
		private int countBikes()
		{
			nbBikes++;
		}
		private int getNbBikes()
		{
			return(nbBikes);
		}
	}
	public void Start ()
	{
		Bike bike1 = new Bike();
		Bike bike2 = new Bike();
		bike1.countBikes();
		bike2.countBikes();
		print("Nb Bikes:"+getNbBikes());

	}
}
```

The following code illustrates the use of static functions.

```
using UnityEngine;
using System.Collections;

public class TestCode : MonoBehaviour {

	public class Bike
	{
		private float speed;
		private int color;
		public static sayHello()
		{
			print ("Hello");
		}
	}
	public void Start ()
	{
		Bike.sayHello();
	}
}
```

The previous code would result in the following output:

```
Hello
```

In the previous code, we declare a static method called **sayHello**; this method is then called in the start method without the need to instantiate (or create) a new **Bike**. This is because, due to its **public** and **static** attributes, it can be accessed from anywhere in the programme.

INHERITANCE

I hope everything is clear so far, as we are going to look at a very interesting and important principle for object-oriented programming: inheritance. The main idea of inheritance is that objects can inherit their properties from other objects (their parent). As they inherit these properties, they can remain identical or evolve and overwrite some of these inherited properties. This is very interesting because it makes it possible to minimize the code by creating a class with general properties for all objects sharing similar features, and then, if need be, to overwrite and customize some of these properties.

Let's take the example of vehicles; they would generally have the following properties:

- Number of wheels.
- Speed.
- Number of passengers.
- Color.
- Capacity to accelerate.
- Capacity to stop.

So we could create the following class for example:

```
class Vehicles
{
	private int nbWheels;
	private float speed;
	private int nbPassengers;
	private int color;
	private void accelerate()
	{
		speed++;
	}
}
```

These features could apply for example to cars, bikes, motorbikes, or trucks. However, all these vehicles also differ; some of them may or may not have an engine or a steering wheel. So we could create a subclass called **MotorizedVehicles**, based on **Vehicles**, but with specificities linked to the fact that they are motorized. These added attributes could be:

- Engine size.
- Petrol type.

- Petrol levels.
- Ability to fill-up the tank.

The following example illustrates how this class could be created.

```
class MotoredVehicles: Vehicles
{
	private float engineSize;
	private int petrolType;
	private float petrolLevels;
	private void fillUpTank()
	{
		petrolLevels+=10;
	}
}
```

- When the class is defined, its name is followed by **: Vehicles**. This means that it inherits from the class **Vehicles**. So it will, by default, avail of all the methods and variables already included in the class **Vehicles**.
- We have created a new member method for this class, called **fillUpTank**.
- In the previous example, you may notice that the methods and variables that were defined for the class **Vehicles** do not appear here; this is because they are implicitly added to this new class, since it inherits from the class **Vehicles**.

Whenever you create a new class in Unity, it will, by default, inherit from the **MonoBehaviour** class; as a result it will implicitly include all the member methods and variables of the class **MonoBehaviour**. Some of these methods include **Start** or **Update**, for example.

> When using inheritance, the parent is usually referred to as the **base class**, while the child is referred to as the **inherited class**.

Now, while the child inherits "Behaviors" from its parents, these can always be modified or, put simply, overwritten. However, in this case, the base method (the method defined in the parent) must be declared as virtual. Also, when overriding this method, the keyword **override** must be used. This is illustrated in the following code.

```
class Vehicles
{
        private int nbWheels;
        private float speed;
        private int nbPassengers;
        private int color;
        private virtual void accelerate()
        {
                speed++;
        }
}
class MotoredVehicles: Vehicles
{
        private float engineSize;
        private int petrolType;
        private float petrolLevels;
        private void fillUpTank()
        {
                petrolLevels+=10;
        }
        private override void accelerate()
        {
                speed+=10;
        }
}
```

In the previous example, while the method **accelerate** is inherited from the class **Vehicles**, it would normally increase the speed by one. However, by overwriting it, we make sure that in the case of objects instantiated from the class **MotoredVehicles**, each acceleration increases the speed by 10.

This point can also be illustrated using some classes in Unity. Let's look at the next example.

```
using UnityEngine;
using System.Collections;

public class TestCode : MonoBehaviour {

      public class Bike
      {
            private float speed;
            private int color;
            public static sayHello()
            {
                  print ("Hello");
            }
      }
      public void Start ()
      {
            Bike.sayHello();
      }
}
```

In this example, we have created a class **TestCode**; this class inherits from **MonoBehaviour**; by default this class includes, amongst other things, a definition for the methods **Start** and **Update**; however, by default, these two methods are blank; this is the reason why we overwrite these methods for the class **TestCode** (inherited from **MonoBehaviour**) so that the **Start** method actually displays some information.

There are obviously more concepts linked to inheritance; however, the information provided in this section should get you started easily. For more information on inheritance in C#, you can look at the official documentation.

METHODS

Methods or functions can be compared to a friend or colleague to whom you gently ask to perform a task, based on specific instructions, and to return the information to you then. For example, you could ask your friend the following: "**Can you please tell me when I will be celebrating my 20th birthday given that I was born in 2000**". So you give your friend (who is good at Math :-)) the information (date of birth) and s/he will calculate the year of your 20th birthday and give this information back to you. So in other words, your friend will be given an input (i.e., the date of birth) and return an output (i.e., the year of your 20th birthday). Methods work exactly this way: they are given information (and sometimes not), perform an action, and then (sometimes, if needed) return information back.

In programming terms, a method (or function) is a block of instructions that performs a set of actions. It is executed when invoked (or put more simply **called**) from the script, or when an event occurs (e.g., the player has clicked on a button or the player collides with an object; we will see more about events in the next section). As for member variables, member functions or methods are declared and they can also be called.

Methods are very useful because once the code for a method has been created, it can be called several times without the need to re-write the same code over and over again. Also, because methods can take parameters, a method can process these parameters and produce or return information accordingly; in other words, they can perform different actions and produce different information based on the input. As a result, methods can do one or all of the following:

- Perform an action.
- Return a result.
- Take parameters and process them.

A method has a syntax and can be declared as follows (in at least two ways).

```
AccessType typeOfdataReturned nameOfTheFunction ()
{
	Perform actions here…
}
```

In the previous code the method does not take any input; neither does it return an output. It just performs actions.

OR

```
AccessType typeOfDataReturned nameOfTheFunction ()
{
      Perform actions here…
}
```

Let's look at the following method for instance.

```
public int calculateSum(int a, int b)
{
      return (a+b);
}
```

In the previous code:

- The method is of type **public**: there are no access restrictions.
- The method will return an integer.
- The name of the method is **calculateSum**.
- The method takes two arguments (i.e., integer parameters).
- The method returns the sum of the two parameters passed (the parameters are referred to as **a** and **b** within this method).

A method can be called using the **()** operator, as follows:

```
nameOfTheFunction1();
nameOfTheFunction2(value);
int test = nameOfTheFunction3(value);
```

In the previous code, a method is called with no parameter (line 1), or with a parameter (line 2). In the third example (line 3), a variable called **test** will be set with the value returned by the method **nameOfTheFunction3**.

> You may, and we will get to this later, have different methods in a class with the exact same name but that take different types of parameters. This is often referred as polymorphism, as the method literally takes different forms and can process information differently based on the information (e.g., type of data) provided.

ACCESSING METHODS AND ACCESS MODIFIERS

As we have seen previously, in C# there are different types of access modifiers. These modifiers specify from where a method can be called and can be **public** (no restricted access), **protected** (access is limited to the containing class or types derived from this class), **internal** (access is limited to the current assembly), **protected internal** (we won't use this access type in this book), and **private** (i.e., access is limited to the containing type).

COMMON METHODS

In Unity, there are many methods available by default, and they are called built-in methods. Some of these functions are called when an event occurs. For example:

- **Start**: called at the start of the scene.
- **Update**: called every time the screen is refreshed.
- **OnControllerColliderHit**: called whenever the **First-Person Controller** (a built-in controller used to make it possible to navigate through your scene using a first-person view) collides with an object.

As we will see later, because most of your classes will inherit by default from the class **MonoBehaviour**, they will, by default, include several methods, including **Start** and **Update** that you will be able to override (i.e., modify for your own use).

Scope of Variables

Whenever you create a variable in C#, you will need to be aware of the scope and access type of the variable so that you use it where its scope makes it possible for you to do so.

The scope of a variable refers to where you can use this variable in a script. In C#, we usually make the difference between **global variables** and **local variables**.

> You can compare the term **local** and **global** variables to a language that is either local or global. In the first case, the local language will only be used (i.e., spoken) by the locals, whereas the global language will be used (i.e., spoken) and understood by anyone whether they are locals or part of the global community.

When you create a class definition along with member variables, these variables will be seen by any method within your class.

Global variables are variables that can be used anywhere in your script, hence the name global. These variables need to be declared at the start of the script (using the usual declaration syntax) and outside of any method; they can then be used anywhere in the script as illustrated in the next code snippet.

```
class MyBike
{
        private int color;
        private float speed;

        public void accelerate()
        {
                speed++;
        }
}
```

In the previous code we declare the variable **speed** as a global variable and access it from the method accelerate.

Local variables are declared within a method and are to be used only within this method, hence the term local, because they can only be used locally, as illustrated in the next code snippet.

```
public void  Start()
{
       int myVar;
       myVar = 0;
}
public void Update()
{
       int myVar2;
       myVar2 = 2;
}
```

In the previous code, **myVar** is a local variable to the method **Start**, and can only be used within this function; **myVar2** is a local variable to the method **Update**, and can only be used within this method.

Events

Throughout this book and in C#, you will read about and use events. So what are they?

Well, put simply, events can be compared to something that happens at a particular time, and when this event occurs, something (e.g., an action) needs to be done. If we make an analogy with daily activities: when the alarm goes off (event) we can either get-up (action) or decide to go back to sleep. When you receive an email (event), you can decide to read it (action), and then reply to the sender (another action).

In computer terms, it is quite similar, although the events that we will be dealing with will be slightly different. So, we could be waiting for the user to press a key (event) and then move the character accordingly (action), or wait until the user clicks on a button on screen (event) to load a new scene (action).

In Unity, whenever an event occurs, a function (or method) is usually called (the function, in this case, is often referred as a handler, because it "handles" the event). You have then the opportunity to modify this function and add instructions (i.e. statements) that should be followed, should this event occur.

To take the analogy of daily activities: we could write instructions to a friend on a piece of paper, so that, in case someone calls in our absence, the friend knows exactly what to do. So an event handler is basically a set of instructions (usually stored within a function) to be followed in case a particular event occurs.

Sometimes information is passed to this method about the particular event, and sometimes not. For example, when the screen is refreshed the method **Update** is called. When the game starts (i.e., when a particular script is enabled), the method **Start** is called. When there is a collision between the player and an object, the method **OnControllerColliderHit** is called. In this particular case (i.e., collision), an object is usually passed to the method that handles the event so that we get to know more about the other object involved in the collision.

As you can see, there can be a wide range of events in our game, and we will get to that later on. In this book, we will essentially be dealing with the following events:

- **Start**: when a script is enabled (e.g., start of the scene).
- **Update**: when the screen is refreshed (e.g., every frame).
- **OnControllerColliderHit**: when a collision occurs between the player and another object.
- **Awake**: when the game starts (i.e., once).

POLYMORPHISM (GENERAL CONCEPTS)

The word polymorphism takes it's meaning from **poly** (several) and **morph** (shape); so it literally means several forms. In object-oriented programming, it refers to the ability to process objects differently (or more specifically) depending on their data type or class. Let's take the example of adding. If we want to add two numbers, we will make an algebraic addition (e.g., 1 + 2). However, adding two **string** variables may mean concatenating them (adding them one after the other). For example adding the text "Hello" and the text "World" would result in the text "**HelloWorld**". As you can see, the way an operation is performed on different data types may vary and produce different results. So again, with polymorphism we will be able to customize methods (or operations) so that data is processed based on its type of class. So, let's look at the following code which illustrates how this can be done in C#.

```
public class AddObjects
{
	public int add (int a, int b)
	{
		return (a + b);
	}
	public string add (string a, string b)
	{
		return (a + b);
	}
}
```

In the previous code, it is possible to add two different types of data: integers and strings. Depending on whether two integers or two strings are passed as parameters, we will be calling either the first **add** method or the second **add** method.

DYNAMIC POLYMORPHISM

In C#, dynamic polymorphism can be achieved using both abstract classes and virtual functions.

In C#, it is possible to create a class that will provide a partial implementation of an interface. Broadly, an interface defines what a class should include (i.e., member methods, member variables or events), but it does not declare how these should be implemented. So, an abstract class will include abstract methods or variables; which means that this class will define the name and type of the variables, the name of the methods, as well as the type of data returned by this method. It is called **abstract** because you cannot implement this type of class (it can never be "materialized"); however, it can be used as a template (or "dream" class) for derived classes. Let's look at the following example.

```
abstract class Vehicule
{
	public abstract void decelerate();
}

class Bike: Vehicule
{
	private float speed;
	private int color;
	public Bike (float newSpeed)
	{
		speed = newSpeed;
	}
	public override void decelerate()
	{
		speed --;
	}
}
```

In the previous code:

- We declare an abstract class **Vehicle**.
- We declare an abstract method called **decelerate**.
- We then create a new class called **Bike**, inherited from the abstract class **Vehicle**.
- We then override the abstract method **decelerate** to use our own implementation.

Using an abstract class just means that we list methods that would be useful for the children; however, the children will have to define how the method should be implemented.

The second way to implement dynamic polymorphism is by using **virtual** methods or variables. In the case of **virtual methods**, we declare a method that will be used by default by objects of this class or inherited classes; however, in this case, even if the method is ready to be used (i.e., because we have defined how it should be implemented), it can be changed (or overridden) by the child (i.e., the inherited class) to fit a specific purpose. In this case (i.e., inherited method), we need to specify that we override this method using the keyword **override**.

The key difference between an abstract and a virtual method is that, while an abstract method should be overridden, a virtual methods may be overridden if the base method (method declared in the base class) does not suit a particular purpose.

Let's look at an example:

```
class Vehicule
{
        private float speed;
        public virtual accelerate()
        {
                speed +=10;
        }
}

class Bike: Vehicule
{
        public override accelerate()
        {
                speed++;
        }
}
```

In the previous code:

- We declare a class **Vehicle**.
- It includes both a private variable **speed** and a virtual method called **accelerate**. This method is virtual, which means that inherited classes will be able to modify (override) it, if need be.
- We then create a new class **Bike** that inherits form the class **Vehicle**. In this class, we override the method accelerate using the keyword **override** so that the speed is just incremented by one.

WORKFLOW TO CREATE A SCRIPT

There are many ways to create and use scripts in Unity, but generally the process is as follows:

- Create a new script using the **Project** view (**Create** | **C# Script)** or the main menu (**Assets** | **Create** | **C# Script**).
- Attach the script to an object (e.g., drag and drop the script on the object).
- Check in the **Console** window that there are no errors in the script.
- Play the scene.

When you create your script, by default, the name of the class within the script will be the name of the script. So let's say that you created a new script called **TestCode**, then the following code will be automatically generated within:

```
using UnityEngine;
using System.Collections;

public class TestCode : MonoBehaviour
{
	public void Start ()
	{
	}
	public void Update ()
	{
	}
}
```

In the previous code, the class **TestCode** has been created; it inherits from the class **MonoBehaviour**, and it includes two methods that can be modified: **Start** and **Update**. You will also notice the two namespaces **UnityEngine** and **System.Collections**. As we have seen earlier, the keywords **using** is called a directive; in this particular case it is used to import what is called a namespace; put simply, by adding this directive you are effectively importing a collection of classes or data types. Each of these namespaces or "libraries" includes useful classes for your programme. For example the namespace **UnityEngine** will include classes for Unity development and **System.Collections** will include classes and interfaces, for different collections of objects. You can of course create classes that will not be linked to any object, and used to instantiate new objects.

HOW SCRIPTS ARE COMPILED

Whenever you create and save a script it is compiled and Unity will notify you (using the **Console** window) of any error. This being said, the order in which the scripts are compiled depends on its location. First, the scripts located in the folders **Standard Assets**, **Pro Standard Assets or Plugins**, then the scripts located in **Standard Assets/Editor**, **Pro Assets/Editor** or **Plugins/Editor**, and then the scripts outside the **Editor** folder, followed by the scripts in the **Editor** folder. For more information on script compilation, you can check the official documentation.

CODING CONVENTION

When you are coding, there are usually naming conventions based on the language that you are using. These often provide increased clarity for your code and depend on the language that you will be using.

Naming conventions usually employ a combination of camel casing and Pascal casing.

- In camel casing all words included in a name, except for the first one, is capitalized (e.g., myVariable).
- In Pascal casing all words included in a name are capitalized (e.g., MyVariable).

When coding in C# for example, naming conventions will use a combinations of camel an Pascal casing depending on whether you are naming a class, an interface, a variable or a resource.

However, as a C# beginner, in addition to learn about classes, methods, or inheritance, it may not be necessary to adhere completely to this naming convention at the start, at least as long as you use a consistent naming scheme.

So, while it is good to acknowledge different naming conventions for programming language and to understand why there are in place, and to keep things simple, this book will use a simplified naming convention, as follows:

- Classes (Pascal casing).
- All methods and variables (camel casing).

Once you feel comfortable with C# and want to know more about the official naming scheme, you may look at Microsoft official naming guidelines.

A FEW THINGS TO REMEMBER WHEN YOU CREATE A SCRIPT (CHECKLIST)

As you create your first scripts in the next chapter, there will be, without a doubt, errors and possibly hair pulling :-). You see, when you start coding, you will, as for any new activity, make small mistakes, learn what they are, improve your coding, and ultimately get better at writing your scripts. As I have seen students learning scripting, there are some common errors that are usually made; these don't make you a bad programmer; on the contrary, it is part of the learning process.

We all learn by trial and error, and making mistakes is part of the learning process.

So, as you create your first script, set any fear aside, try to experiment, be curious, and get to learn the language. It is like learning a new foreign language: when someone from a foreign country understands your first sentences, you feel so empowered! So, it will be the same with C#, and to ease the learning process, I have included a few tips and things to keep in mind when writing your scripts, so that you progress even faster. You don't need to know all of these by now (I will refer to these later on, in the next chapter), but just be aware of it and also use this list if any error occurs (this list is also available as a pdf file in the resource pack, so that you can print it and keep it close by). So, watch out for these :-).

- Each opening bracket has a corresponding closing bracket.
- All variables are written consistently (e.g., spelling and case). The name of each variable is case-sensitive; this means that if you declare a variable **myvariable** but then refer to it as **myVariable** later on in the code, this may trigger an error, as the variable **myVariable** and **myvariable**, because they have a different case (upper- or lower-case **V**), are seen as two different variables.
- All variables are declared (type and name) prior to being used (e.g., **int**).
- The type of the argument passed to a method is the type that is required by this method.
- The type of the argument returned by a method is the type that is required to be returned by this method.
- Built-in functions are spelt with the proper case (e.g., upper-case **U** for **Update**).
- Use **camel casing** (i.e., capitalize the first character of each word except for the first word) or **Pascal casing** (i.e., capitalize the first character of each word) consistently.
- All statements are ended with a semi-colon.
- For **if** statements the condition is within round brackets.
- For **if** statements the condition uses the syntax "==" rather than "=".

- When calling a method, the exact name of this method (i.e., case-sensitive) is used.
- When referring to a variable, it is done with regards to the access type of the variable (e.g., public or private).
- Local variables are declared and can be used within the same method.
- Global variables are declared outside methods and can be used anywhere within the class.

Level Roundup

Summary

In this chapter, we have become familiar with C# and different programming concepts. We also looked into object-oriented programming. In the next chapter, we will harness these skills to be able to create (and execute) our first script.

Quiz

It is now time to test your knowledge. Please answer the following questions. The answers are available in the resource pack.

1. The following statement will print the text **Hello World** in the **Console** window.

```
print("Hello World");
```

2. The value of the variable **c** in the following statement will be **3**.

```
int a;
int b;
a = 1;
b =1;
c = a + b;
```

3. The value of the variable **fullName**, in the following code snippet, will be **JohnPaul**.

```
string fName = "John";
string lName = "Paul";
string fullName = fName + lName;
```

4. The following code snippet will print **I will not go sailing**.

```
bool windIsStrong;
windIsStrong = true;
if (windIsStrong) print ("I will not go sailing");
```

5. The following code snippet will print **I will not go sailing**.

```
bool weatherIsSunny;
bool windIsStrong;
bool iWillGoSailing;
weatherIsSunny = true;
windIsStrong = false;
If (weatherIsSunny && !windIsStrong ) print ("I will go sailing");
If (!weatherIsSunny || windIsStrong ) print ("I will not go sailing");
```

6. Spot three coding mistakes in the following snippet.

```
int test
int test2;
test3 = 0;
test 3 = test1 + test2;
```

7. Consider the method described in the next code snippet, and select the correct way to call it (i.e., A, B, or C):

a) **displayMessage();**
b) **displayAMessage()**
c) **displayAMessage();**

```
public void displayAMessage()
{
}
```

8. The value of the variable **counter** in the following code snippet will be **3** after the code has been executed.

```
int counter;
counter = 0;
counter = counter + 1;
```

9. The following code will print the message **Hello** every second.

```
public void Update()
{
      print ("Hello");
}
```

10. A local variable can be used from any part of a script.

Checklist

If you can do the following, then you are ready to proceed to the next chapter:

- Understand the concept of classes.
- Know how to call a method
- List and understand at least three types of variables in C#.
- Understand the difference between **private** and **public** variables.
- Answer at least 7 out of 10 of the questions correctly in the quiz.

2

CREATING YOUR FIRST SCRIPT

In this section we will start to code C# scripts in Unity. Some of the objectives of this section will be to:

- Introduce C# scripting in Unity.
- Explain some basic scripting concepts.
- Explain how to display information from the code to the **Console** window.

After completing this chapter, you will be able to:

- Understand basic concepts in C#.
- Understand best coding practices.
- Code your first script in Unity.
- Create classes, methods and variables.
- Instantiate objects based on your own classes.
- Use built-in methods.
- Use conditional statements.

You can skip this chapter if you are already familiar with C#, or if you have already created and used C# scripts within Unity.

QUICK OVERVIEW OF THE INTERFACE

Throughout this book you will be using different windows in Unity; each of these windows includes a label (usually in the top-left corner of the window), and all can be moved around, if necessary, by either changing the layout (**Window | Layouts | …**) or by dragging and dropping the corresponding tab for a window (this will move the view to where you would like it to appear within the window). In the default layout, the following views appear onscreen (as described in the next screenshot, clockwise from the top left corner):

1. The **Hierarchy** window (the corresponding shortcut is *CTRL+4*): this window (or view) lists all the objects currently present in your scene; these could include, for example, basic shapes, 3D characters, or terrains. This view also makes it possible to identify a hierarchy between objects; for example, we can see in this view if some objects have children or parents (we will explore this concept later).

2. The **Scene** view (*CTRL+1*): this window displays the content of a scene (or the item listed in the **Hierarchy** view) so that you can visualize them and modify them accordingly using the mouse (e.g., move, scale, etc.).

3. The **Game** view (*CTRL+2*): this window makes it possible to visualize the scene as it will appear in the game (i.e., through the lenses of the active camera).

4. The **Inspector** view (*CTRL+3*): this window displays information (i.e., properties) on the object currently selected.

5. The **Console** window (*SHIFT+CTRL+C*): this window displays messages either printed from the code by the user (using keywords) or by Unity. These include warnings or error messages related to your project or code.

6. The **Project** window (*CTRL+5*): this window includes all the assets available and used for your project. These include 3D models, sounds, or textures.

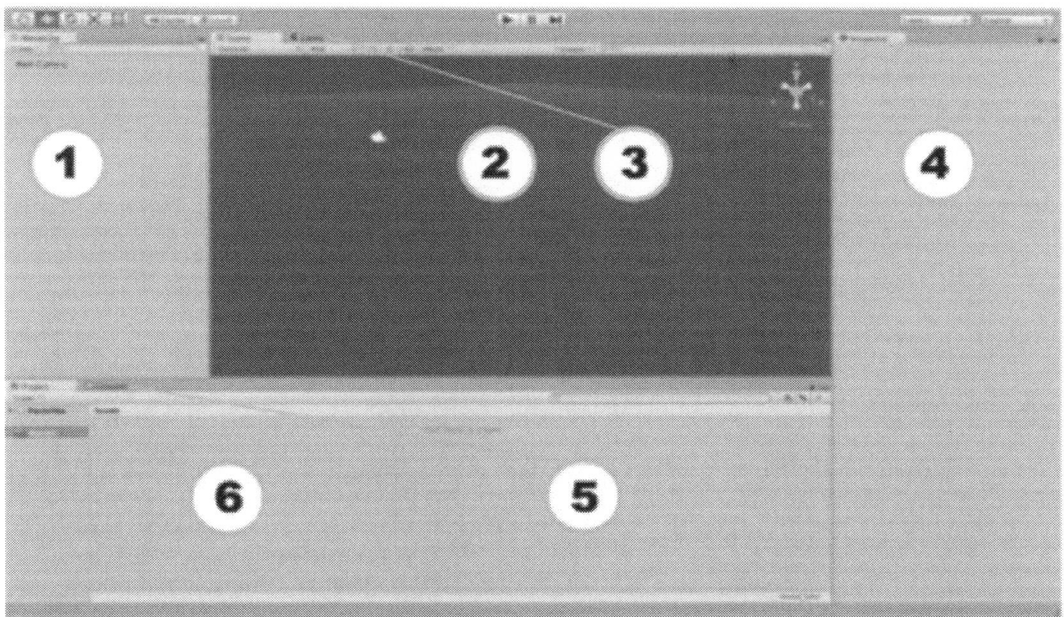

Figure 2-1: Main windows and views in Unity

If you need to know more about how to use common views and shortcuts in Unity, you may download the first book in the series: Unity 5 from Zero to Proficiency (Foundations).

GETTING STARTED

In Unity, a script (C# script) is usually linked to an object; although it can also be used as a standalone class to be instantiated at a later stage; generally, for your script to be executed, it will need to be linked to an object. So to start with, we will create an empty object, create a script, and link this script to the object.

- Please launch Unity.
- Create a new Project (**File | New Project**).
- Create a new scene (**File | New Scene**).
- Create an empty object (**GameObject | Create Empty**).
- Rename this object: **example_for_scripting** in the **Hierarchy** window. To do so, you can either right-click on this object and then select the option **Rename**, from the contextual menu, or select the object (i.e., click once on it) and press *CTRL + Enter*.
- You will notice, looking at the **Inspector** window, that this object has only one component (**Transform**).

Let's create a new script:

- In the **Project** window, click once on the **Assets** folder.
- Create a new folder to store the scripts (this is not compulsory but it will help to organize your scripts): Select **Create | Folder**.

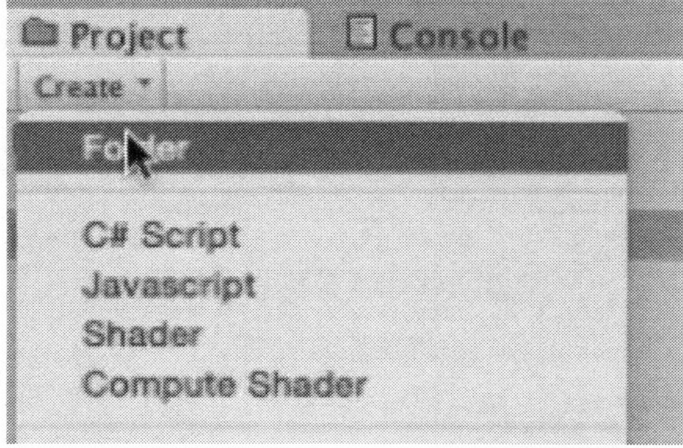

Figure 2-2: Creating a new folder

- This will create a new folder labeled **Folder**.

- Rename this folder **Scripts**.
- Double click on this folder to display its content and so that the script that we are about to create is added to this folder.
- In the **Project** window, select **Create | C# Script**.
- This should create a new **C#** script.

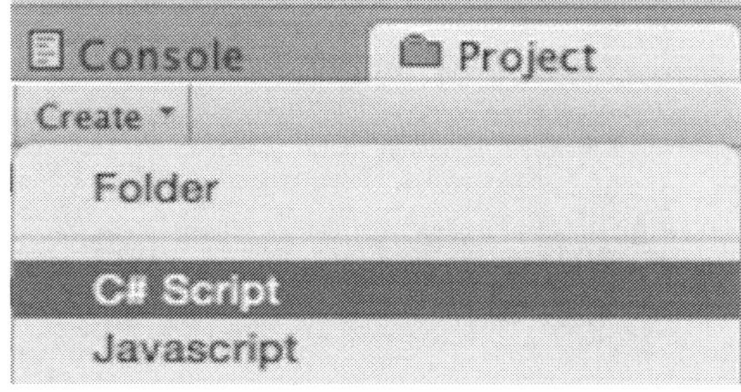

Figure 2-3: Creating a new C# script

- By default, this script will be named **NewBehaviourScript**. However, the name will be highlighted in blue so that you modify the name before the content of the script is created. Please rename this script **MyFirstScript**.

Note that the name of the script should always match the name of the main class within the script; so if you want to rename this script later on, you will also need to modify the name of the main class within the script.

- Click once on the script; as you do so, look at the **Inspector** window, and you will see the content of the script. By default, you will notice that it includes a definition for the class **MyFirstScript**, namespaces, as well as two different member methods **Start** and **Update**.
- Double-click on the script (within the **Project** window), this will open the script in **MonoDevelop**, which is the default editor for Unity.

Note that you can change to the editor of your choice (e.g., Notepad++ or Sublime). This can be done by changing Unity's preferences (**Edit | Preferences | External Tool**). This being said, while Mono Develop provides code auto completion by default, this may not be the case for other code editors (e.g., with Sublime, you need to install a specific package).

- As the script is opened in Mono Develop we can see it in more detail. Again, the **Start** method is called at the start of the scene, once. The method **Update** is called every time the screen is refreshed (every frame).

- These functions are case-sensitive; because they are built-in functions (i.e., functions made available by Unity for your use), Unity is expecting them to be spelt with the exact spelling and case; otherwise, it will assume that the method that you write serves a different purpose (i.e., we will come back to this type of error later-on).

So let's start coding.

- First let's create a variable of type **integer** called **number** as a private member variable.
- Type the following code just before the method **Start**:

```
private int number;
```

- As you can see, the variable is declared outside any method but inside the class **MyFirstScript**, which means that it is a member variable. The access modifier **private** specifies that the variable is accessible only by the class **MyFirstScript**.
- Then, we can declare a **String** variable called **myName**. Type the following code just after the previous declaration.

```
private string myName;
```

- Then type the following code inside the method **Start** (i.e., anywhere within its curly brackets).

```
number = 1;
```

- This code sets the variable **number** to 1; this variable was declared at the start of the script, as a member variable and it can be accessed from anywhere within the class **MyFirstScript**, including from inside the method **Start**.
- Then type the following code inside the method **Start** after the previous statement (you can replace the word **Patrick** with your own name if you wish):

```
myName = “Patrick”;
```

- As you type this line, make sure that the name of the variable is spelt properly with proper case (i.e., upper-case **N**).
- Then type the following code after the previous statement to display a message in the **Console** window.

```
print ("Hello" + myName + "Your number is "+number);
```

- This should print the message **"Hello Patrick Your number is 1"** in the **Console** window in Unity. This window displays error messages from Unity or messages from the code. You may notice the quotes around the word **Patrick**, this means that the text **Hello** will be displayed and we will add the value of the variable **myName** to it. So these two strings will be concatenated (i.e., grouped) to form a dynamic sentence for which the content will depend on the value of the variables **myName** and **number**.

So at this stage, your code should look as follows (and if it doesn't, you can use the next code snippet as a template):

```
using UnityEngine;
using System.Collections;
public class MyFirstScript : MonoBehaviour
{
	// Use this for initialization
	private int number;
	private string name;
	void Start ()
	{
		number = 1;
		myName = "Patrick";
		print ("Hello"+ myName + "Your number is "+number);
	}
	// Update is called once per frame
	void Update ()
	{

	}
}
```

- At this stage, we can save our script (*CTRL + S*) and go back to Unity (*ALT + TAB*).
- In Unity, drag and drop the script **MyFirstScript** onto the empty object **example_for_scripting**, as illustrated on the next figure.

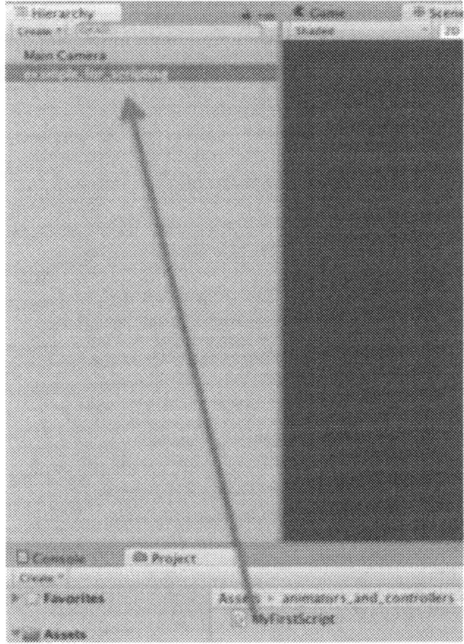

Figure 2-4: Linking the script to an object

- After this, if you click on the object **example_for_scripting** in the hierarchy, you should now see in the **Inspector** window that the script has become a component of this object.
- Look at the **Console** window to see if there are any errors; the window should be empty (i.e., no errors). If there are any warnings, you can leave them for the time being (it won't stop the scene from playing).
- We can now play the scene (*CTRL + P*); as we play the scene and look at the **Console** window (*SHIFT + CTRL + C*), we should see the message "**Hello Patrickyour number is 1**".

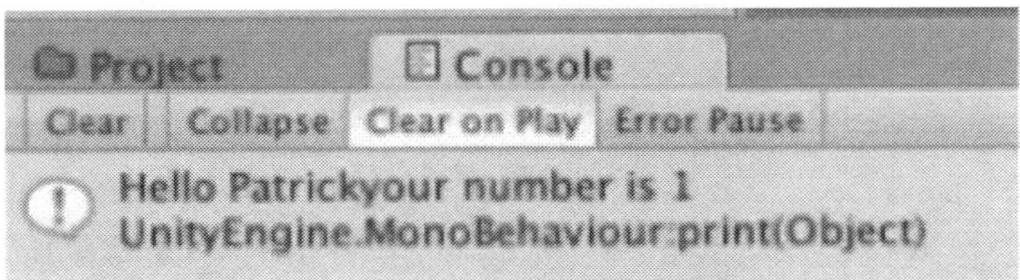

Figure 2-5: Displaying a message in the Console window - part 1

- You may notice a missing space between the words **Patrick** and **you**, and we can correct this accordingly. To do so, we can go back to your code editor (e.g., **Mono Develop**) to modify the script and add spaces as follows (after the words **Hello** and **is,** and before the word **your**):

```
print("Hello " + myName + " your number is "+number);
```

As we go back to Unity, we can clear the **Console** window by clicking on the tab called **Clear**, as highlighted on the next figure. However, so that the **Console** window is cleared every time we run the scene, we can also click on the tab labeled **Clear on Play**. This ensures that the **Console** window is cleared every time the scene is played, avoiding cluttering the **Console** window with messages that may be obsolete or irrelevant.

- As we play the scene, we can see that the message has been modified to include a space between the words **Patrick** and **your**.

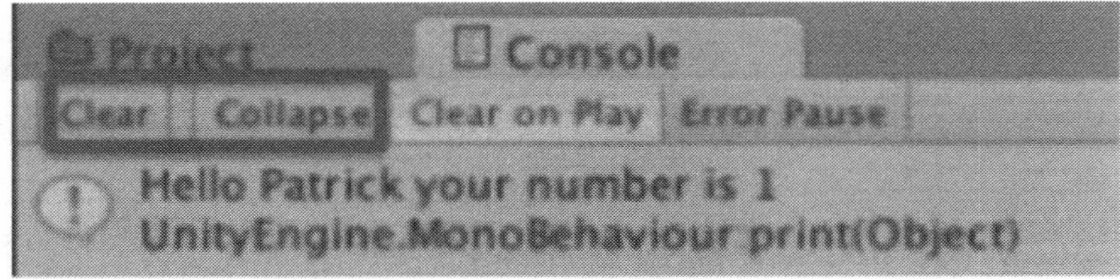

Figure 2-6: Displaying a message in the console window - part 2

This is it! We have created our first script using the built-in method **Start** and some variables, more specifically global variables. These variables are of type **integer** and **String**. Again, these variables are global as they were declared at the start of the script and outside any method. They can, as a result, be used across the script. The full script should look as described on the next code snippet.

```
using UnityEngine;
using System.Collections;
public class MyFirstScript : MonoBehaviour
{
	// Use this for initialization
	private int number;
	private string myName;

	void Start ()
	{
		number = 1;
		myName = "Patrick";
		print("Hello "+ myName + "Your number is " +number);
	}
	// Update is called once per frame
	void Update ()
	{

	}
}
```

USING THE UPDATE FUNCTION

Let's now use the method **Update** to display another message in the **Console** window. Again, this method is called every frame (i.e., every time the screen is refreshed), so any message printed within this method will be displayed indefinitely and every frame.

- Switch to Unity.
- Double click on the script **MyFirstScript** to open it.
- In **Mono Develop** (or any other code editor of your choice), type the following code within the curly brackets of the method **Update**:

```
print (myName);
```

- Save your code (*CTRL + S* or *APPLE + S* for Mac users).
- Switch to Unity and play the scene (*CTRL + P*).

- You should see that the message **Patrick** (or your own name) is displayed indefinitely. In the next figure, we can see that the message is displayed 148 times after a few seconds.

Figure 2-7: Using the "Collapse" option – part 1

- So the code is working well; however, because the message is displayed so many times, we have lost sight of the first message displayed from the **Start** function. This is because the console is flooded by hundreds of identical messages, and we could, to clear up the console, click on the tab labeled **Collapse** within the **Console** window.

The **Collapse** option ensures that identical messages are displayed only once, along with a number that indicates how many times they have been listed.

- If we stop the game, press the **Collapse** option, and play the scene again, the **Console** window should look as described in the following figure.

Figure 2-8: Using the "Collapse" option - part 2

- As we can see, the message from the **Start** method is displayed (once), whereas the message from the **Update** method is displayed once but the consoles indicates that it has been issued 223 times.

CREATING LOCAL VARIABLES

At this stage, the code is working well, and we have created two member variables: **number** and **myName**. These two variables are accessible throughout our class; however, to experiment with local variables, we could also create variables that are only accessible from one method. So let's experiment.

- Switch back to your code editor (e.g., Mono Develop).
- Delete or comment the code we have just created in the **Start** function. To comment code, you can use double forward slashes, as described in the next code snippet.

```
//print (myName);
```

- Add the following code to the method **Start**, just before the closing bracket for this function.

```
int localVariable = 3;
print("local variable: "+localVariable);
```

With the first statement, we declare a variable that should only be used locally, that is to say, within the method **Start**. We then print the value of this variable and display a message that includes the string **"local variable"** that will be followed by (or appended to) the value of the variable **localVariable**; in our case, this should display **"local variable: 3"**.

- Check the code that you have written and ensure that it is correct (e.g., semi-colon at the end of each line).
- Save your script.
- Switch back to Unity and play the scene.
- As we play the scene, the **Console** window should look like the following:

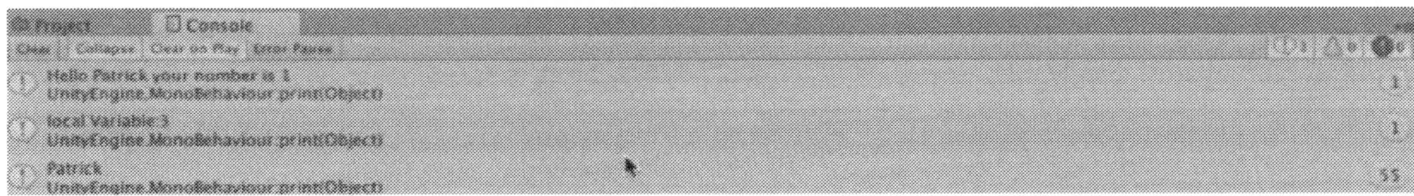

Figure 2-9: Displaying a local variable in the Console window

- We can see the first message from the **Start** method along with the second message that we have just created. Then the message from the **Update** method is displayed (55 times at this stage).
- Now, just to demonstrate the importance of variable scope, we will make an error on purpose; we will try to use the variable **myVariable** (which is a local variable) outside the method **Start**, where it has initially been declared. As you may have guessed, this should trigger an error.
- Switch back to **Mono Develop**.
- Type or copy and paste the following code inside the method **Update**.

```
print("local variable: "+localVariable);
```

- Save your script (*CTRL + S*).
- Switch back to Unity. Before you can try to play the scene, you will notice an error in the **Console** window as follows.

Figure 2-10: Generating an error on purpose

> By displaying this message, Unity is telling us that it does not recognize the variable **localVariable** in the context where it is being used. This is because it was declared locally in the **Start** method and then used outside this method. So if you see similar messages as you code your game, always check the scope of your variable. This should save you some headaches. :-)

- Switch back to your code editor and comment or delete the line we just created in the **Update** method.

```
//print("local variable "+localVariable);
```

> In C# you can comment a line of code by adding // to the start of the line. This means that the code will be part of the script, but it will not be executed.

CREATING A SIMPLE COUNTER

Let's create a simple counter to practice declaring and assigning values to variables. This timer will just count from 0 onwards and use a variable for which the value will be increased overtime (i.e., every frame).

- Switch back to **MonoDevelop** by pressing *ALT + Tab (or CMD + Tab* for Mac users*)*.

> As you will have to switch from Unity to **Mono Develop** (or another code editor) a couple of times during development, you can use this shortcut to do so, and it will save you a good bit of time. Imagine saving three seconds 300 times a day! So by pressing *ALT + Tab* (or *APPLE + Tab* on a Mac computer) you can switch back to the previous window (or the application that you were using). By keeping *ALT* pressed and then successively pressing the tab key several times, you can see and select the applications that are currently running on your computer.

- Add the following line at the top of our class (i.e., **MyFirstScript**) to declare our counter (just after the declaration for **myName**).

```
private int counter;
```

- Then, initialize the variable **counter** to **zero** by adding the following code within the **Start** method.

```
counter = 0;
```

Note that this is done in the **Start** method only for now, so that it is done only once (i.e., at the start of the scene). If we were to add this code to the **Update** method instead, the variable would be initialized to 0 every frame (constantly), and we don't want this right now.

- Finally, add the following code at the end of the **Update** method so that we add one to the current value of the variable **counter** every frame (i.e., every time the screen is refreshed) and display its value.

```
counter = counter + 1;
print ("counter="+counter);
```

- After you have made these modifications, the code should look as follows:

```
using UnityEngine;
using System.Collections;
public class MyFirstScript : MonoBehaviour
{
	// Use this for initialization
	private int number;
	private string myName;
	private int counter;

	void Start ()
	{
		number = 1;
		myName = "Patrick";
		print("Hello "+ myName + "Your number is " +number);

		int localVariable = 3;
		print("local variable: "+localVariable);
		counter = 0;
	}

	// Update is called once per frame
	void Update ()
	{
		counter = counter + 1;
		print ("counter="+counter);
	}
}
```

- Switch back to Unity (*ALT* + *TAB*).

- Look at the **Console** window: it should not display any error (i.e., provided that you have commented or deleted the code that we created to generate an error on purpose).
- Play the scene (*CTRL* + *P*), look at the **Console** window, and you should see that the value of the counter is displayed and that it is increasing.

You may notice that, even if you press the **Collapse** option in the **Console** window, the messages are not collapsed and that they still flood the **Console** window. This is because the **Collapse** option works only when the exact same message is displayed several times; however, in our case, the message differs every frame as the value of the counter is different every time (e.g., "counter=1", "counter=2", etc.).

At this stage we know about local and global variables, so let's look into methods and create our very first method.

CREATING YOUR FIRST METHOD

So what is a method? A method (what we used to call function in JavaScript) is usually employed to perform a task outside the main body of the game. I usually compare functions to a friend or a colleague to whom you gently ask to perform a task for you. In many cases you will call them and they will perform the task. Sometime they will need some particular information to perform the task (e.g., a number to be able to call someone on your behalf); some other times, they will call you back to give you the information that they found, but in other cases, this may not be necessary, and they will perform the task without contacting you afterwards.

So there are essentially three types of methods:

- Methods that just perform actions with no parameters.
- Methods that perform actions with parameters.
- Methods that perform actions (with or without a parameter) and return a result.

DECLARING A METHOD

If you have coded in JavaScript before, functions were declared using the keyword **function**; however, in C# a method declaration usually requires an access modifier, the type of data returned, and the type of the parameters passed to this function.

The syntax to declare a method is as follows:

- The access modifier (e.g., private, public, or protected).
- The type of data returned by the method (e.g., **float**, **string** or **bool**).
- The name of the method.
- Opening round brackets.
- The type of the parameters and their name.
- Closing round brackets.
- Any action (i.e., statement) performed by this method will be added within the curly brackets and followed by a semi-colon.

In the next sections, we will see examples of how methods can be declared.

METHODS THAT DON'T RETURN OR TAKE ANY PARAMETER

In this case, the method is called with no parameter; it will then perform an action. This is the simplest form of methods. The syntax is as follows: the access modifier, the keyword **void**, followed by the **name of the function**, followed by **opening and closing round brackets**, followed by **opening and closing curly brackets**. Any action (i.e., statement) performed by this function will be added within the curly brackets and followed by a semi-colon.

```
public void theNameOfyourMethod()
{
}
```

The keyword **void** indicates that the method does not return any data.

So to create our first method, we could type the following at the end of our script (i.e., before the last closing curly brackets):

```
public void myFirstMethod()
{
      print ("Hello World");
}
```

When called, this method will print the message **"Hello World"** to the **Console** window.

At this stage we have just defined the method **myFirstMethod**; in other words, we have specified what the method should do when it has been called. So once the method has been defined, we can call it using the syntax: **nameOfTheMethod();** for example, to call **myFirstMethod** from any other method within the script, we could write the following statement at the end of the **Start** method:

```
myFirstMethod();
```

So that this message stands out in the **Console** window, we can comment all other **print** statements inside the **Start** method so that the code of your script looks like this (the changes are highlighted in bold):

```
using UnityEngine;
using System.Collections;
public class MyFirstScript : MonoBehaviour
{
	// Use this for initialization
	private int number;
	private string myName;
	private int counter;

	void Start ()
	{
		number = 1;
		myName = "Patrick";
		//print("Hello "+ myName + "Your number is " +number);

		int localVariable = 3;
		//print("local variable: "+localVariable);
		counter = 0;
		myFirstMethod();
	}

	// Update is called once per frame
	void Update ()
	{
		counter = counter + 1;
		//print ("counter="+counter);

	}
	public void myFirstMethod()
	{
		print ("Hello World");
	}
}
```

You may wonder why the methods **Update** and **Start** do not include any access modifier (e.g., public or private). This is because by default, the access modifier for a member method in C# is private. So if no access modifier is specified for a method, it will be treated as a private method.

Note that the location of the method in the script (i.e., at the end or at the start) does not matter, as long as it is declared within the class (**MyFirstScript**) and outside any another method: so you need to declare your method outside of any other methods (i.e., after the closing curly bracket for a method or before the method); we could have easily written this method at the start or middle of the script, resulting in no errors.

- Check that your code is written properly (i.e., error-free).
- Save your code (*CTRL + S*).
- Switch to Unity (*ALT + TAB*).
- Check that there are no errors in the **Console** window.
- Play the scene and check that the message says **"Hello World"**.

DEFINING A METHOD THAT TAKES PARAMETERS

So far, we looked at methods that would not take or return any parameters. For now, we will create a method that still doesn't return any data, but that takes one or several parameters in order to perform calculations.

So to borrow the previous example, you call someone, give them some information, and ask them to perform an action based on your instructions. To illustrate this concept, let's create a new method that will display a message based on a parameter passed as an argument.

- Please type the following code at the end of the class (i.e., before the last closing curly bracket).

```
public void mySecondMethod(string name)
{
	print ("Hello, your name is " +name);
}
```

- In the previous code, we have created a method called **mySecondMethod**. It takes a parameter called **name** of type **String** (i.e., text). So when we call this method and include a string variable within the brackets, this variable will be referred as **name** within this method.
- Let me illustrate with the following code.

```
mySecondMethod("Patrick");
```

If we were to type the previous code inside the **Start** method, the method **mySecondMethod** would set the variable **name** with the string **Patrick**, and then display the message **Hello Patrick**. The variable **name** is a local variable to the method **mySecondFunction**.

If you have not already done so, please add the following code to the **Start** method. You can replace the word **Patrick** with your own name.

```
mySecondMethod("Patrick");
```

- Save your code, switch to Unity, check the **Console** window for any error and play the scene.
- You should see, amongst other messages, the message **"Hello, your name is Patrick"**.
- You could now change the call to this method and pass your own name as a parameter and see the result as you play the scene.

Note that we could have created a method that takes many other parameters. For example, we could have created a method that takes the first and last names as parameters, as follows.

```
public void myThirdMethod(string fName, string lName)
{
      print ("Hello, your name is " +fName+" "+lName);
}
```

DEFINING A METHOD THAT TAKES PARAMETERS AND RETURNS INFORMATION

So far we know how to declare a method that takes parameters; however we have not yet seen how we could define a method that also returns information.

This type of method, will, in addition to possibly taking parameters and processing this information, return information back to where it was called.

In the following example, we will create a method that does all three: it will be called; it will then take the **year of birth** as a parameter, and then calculate and return the corresponding **age** (based on the current year).

- Please add the following code at the end of the script.

```
public int calculateAge(int YOB)
{
        int age;
        age = 2016 - YOB;
        return (age);
}
```

In the previous code:

- The method called **calculateAge** is declared using the keywords **public** and **int** as its access type is **public** and as it will return an **integer**.
- The method called **calculateAge** takes a parameter called **YOB** (short for Year Of Birth).
- The method **calculateAge** then subtracts **YOB** from the current year and returns the result.

Please add the following code to the method **Start**.

```
int myAge = calculateAge(1998);
print("Your age is " + myAge);
```

In the previous code:

- The method **calculateAge** is called once; it returns the calculated age, and this (returned) value is saved in the variable called **myAge**.
- This variable **myAge** is then printed in the **Console** window.
- Save your code, and switch back to Unity.
- Check that there are no errors in the **Console** window and play the scene.
- The console should display, amongst other messages, the message **"Your age is 18"**.

As you can see, there are different types of methods that you can create, depending on your needs. They may or may not take parameters, and they may or may not return values.

CREATING YOUR OWN CLASS

To complete this section, it would be great to see how you could create and use your own class. So, we will simply create a class for a bike and also use it. So, let's get started.

- Please create a new C# script called **Bike** (i.e., select **Create | C# Script** from the **Project** window).
- This should generate a script with the following code by default:

```
using UnityEngine;
using System.Collections;

public class Bike : MonoBehaviour {

	// Use this for initialization
	void Start () {

	}

	// Update is called once per frame
	void Update () {

	}
}
```

When this is done, let's edit this script to add some features to our bike.

- We can start by deleting the text **:MonoBehaviour**. This is because our class will be used as a standalone and not inherit from the **MonoBehaviour** class (which is mainly for game objects in the scene).
- Then we can delete the methods Start and Update, for the same reason as explained above, as we will create our own methods for our class Bike.
- So your code should look like the following:

```
using UnityEngine;
using System.Collections;

public class Bike
{


}
```

At this stage we have a blank canvas that we can use for our new class.

- Please add the following code at the start of the class (just before the comment "**Use this for initialization**"). The new code is highlighted in bold.

```
using UnityEngine;
using System.Collections;

public class Bike
{

        private string name;
        private float speed;
        private int nbWheels;

}
```

- In the previous code, we declare three private member variables of type **string**, **float** and **int**. These will be used to identify the name, speed and number of wheels for the bike created.

We now need to define one or more constructors for our class, to define the feature of each new bike created. Please add the following code within the class:

```
//First Constructor
public Bike()
{
      name = "Just another bike";
      speed = 0.0f;
}
//Second Constructor
public Bike(string newName)
{
      name = newName;
      speed = 0.0f;
      Debug.Log ("Just created a new bike with the name" + name);

}
```

- In the previous code, we create two constructors; both methods are public and their names are the same as the name of our class (i.e., Bike).

The method **print** that we used earlier is only accessible for classes that inherit from the class **MonoBehaviour**; in our case, we have removed this inheritance (our class does not inherit anymore from the class **MonoBehaviour**), so we use the method **Debug.Log** instead which is accessible from the library **UnityEngine** that we imported at the start of our script); this is equivalent to the method **print**.

- The first constructor will be used if the object is created but no parameters are used at its instantiation. We see that, by default, we just set the name of this bike to "**Just another bike**" and its speed to **0**. This constructor will be called if we use the following code to create a new bike.

```
Bike bike1 = new Bike();
```

- The next constructor takes a **string** as a parameter; which means that it will be called if we create a new bike and pass a string as a parameter when an object is created from this class (i.e., instantiated). We see that if this is the case, the name of the bike will be set to (or initialized with) the parameter passed to this constructor and its speed will be set to **0**. This constructor will be called if we use the following code to create a new bike.

```
Bike bike2 = new Bike("Name of the Bike");
```

So your code should look like the following by now (if not, you can use the next code as a template).

```
using UnityEngine;
using System.Collections;

public class Bike
{
	private string name;
	private float speed;
	private int nbWheels;

	//First Constructor
	public Bike()
	{
		name = "Just another bike";
		speed = 0.0f;
	}
	//Second Constructor
	public Bike(string newName)
	{
		name = newName;
		speed = 0.0f;
		Debug.Log ("Just created a new bike with the name " + name);
	}
}
```

So, once you have created our new class, we could now test it by doing the following:

- Open the script **MyFirstScript**.
- Add the following code in the **Start** method.

```
Bike b1 = new Bike ("My First Bike");
```

- Save your script.
- Play the scene.
- You should see that the **Console** window displays the message **"Just created a new bike with the name My First Bike"**.

So at this stage, while we have created constructors, we could also create methods that make it possible to modify some of the attributes of our bike.

For example, we could add the following method to the class **Bike**.

```
public void accelerate ()
{
        speed+=1;
        Debug.Log ("Our new speed is now" + speed);
}
```

We can then modify the **Start** method in the script MyFirstScript as follows (new code in bold).

```
Bike b1 = new Bike ("My First Bike");
b1.accelerate();
b1.accelerate();
```

Save this code, and play the scene. You should see two additional messages in the **Console** window saying **"Our new speed is now 1"** and **"Our new speed is now 2"**.

COMMON ERRORS AND THEIR MEANING

As you will start your journey through C# coding, you may sometimes find it difficult to interpret the errors produced by Unity in the console. However, after some practice, you will manage to recognize them, to understand (and also avoid) them, and to fix them accordingly. The next list identifies the errors that my students often come across when they start coding in C#.

When an error occurs, Unity usually provides you with enough information to check where it has occurred, so that you can fix it. While many are relatively obvious to spot, some others are trickier to find. In the following, I have listed some of the most common errors that you will come across as you start with C#. The trick is to recognize the error message so that you can understand what Unity is trying to tell you. Again, this is part of the learning process, and you **WILL** make these mistakes, but as you see these errors, you will learn to understand them (and avoid them too :-)). Again, Unity is trying to help you by communicating, to the best that it can, where the issue is; by understanding the error messages we can get to fix these bugs easily. So that it is easier to fix errors, Unity usually provides the following information when an error occurs:

- Name of the script where the error was found.
- The number of the row and column where the error was found.
- A description of the error that was found.

So, if Unity was to generate the following message **"Assets/Scripts/MyFirstScript.cs (23,34) BCE0085: Unknown identifier: 'localVariable'"**, it is telling us that an error has occurred in the script called **MyFirstScript**, at the line **23**, and around the **34th** character (i.e., column) on this line. In this particular message, it is telling us that it can't recognize the variable **localVariable**.

So, you may come across the following errors (this list is also available in the resource pack as a pdf file, so that you can print it and keep it close by):

- **";" expected**: This error could mean that you have forgotten to add a semi-colon at the end of a statement. To fix this error, just go to the line mentioned in the error message and ensure that you add a semi-colon.
- **Unknown identifier**: This error could mean that Unity does not know the variable that you are mentioning. It can be due to at least three reasons: (1) the variable has not been declared yet, (2) the variable has been declared but outside the scope of the method (e.g., declared locally in a different function), or (3) the name of the variable that you are using is incorrect (i.e., spelling or case). Remember, the names of all variables and functions are case-sensitive; so by just using an incorrect case, Unity will assume that you refer to another variable, which, in this case, has not been declared yet.
- **The best method overload for function ... is not compatible**: This error is probably due to the fact that you are trying to call a function and to pass a parameter with a type

that is not what Unity is expecting. For example, the method **mySecondMethod**, described in the next code snippet, is expecting a **String** value for its parameter; so, if you pass an integer value instead, an error will be generated.

```
void mySecondFunction(string name)
{
        print ("Hello, your name is" +name);
}
mySecondFunction("John");//this is correct
mySecondFunction(10);//this will trigger an error
```

- **Expecting } found ...:** This error is due to the fact that you may have forgotten to either close or open curly brackets. This can be the case for conditional statements or functions. To avoid this issue, there is a trick (or best practice) that you can use: you can ensure that you indent your code so that corresponding opening and closing brackets are at the same level. In the next example, you can see that the brackets corresponding to the start and end of the method **testBrackets** are indented at the same level, and so are the brackets for each of the conditional statements within this function. By indenting your code (using several spaces or tabulation), you can make sure that your code is clear and that missing curly brackets are easier to spot.

```
Void testBrackets()
{
        if (myVar == 2)
        {
                print ("Hello World");
                myVar = 4;
        }
        else
        {
        }
}
```

Sometimes, although the syntax of your code is correct and does not yield any error in the **Console** window, it looks like nothing is happening; in other words, it looks like the code, and especially the methods that you have created do not work. This is bound to happen as you create your first scripts. It can be quite frustrating (and I have been there :-)) because, in this case, Unity will not let us know where the error is. However, there is a succession of checks that you can perform to ensure that this does not happen; so you could check the following:

- The script that you have written has been saved.
- The script has no errors.
- The script is attached to an object.
- If the script is indeed attached to an object and you are using a built-in method that depends on the type of object it is attached to, make sure that the script is linked to the correct object. For example, if your script is using the built-in method

OnControllerColliderHit, which is used to detect collision between the **FPSController** and other objects, but you don't drag and drop the script on the **FPSController** object, the script, while being error-free, will not be used, and the method **OnControllerColliderHit** will not be called if you collide with an object.

- If the script is indeed attached to the right object and is using a built-in method such as **Start**, or **Update**, make sure that these functions are spelt properly (i.e., exact spelling and case). For example for the method **Update**, what happens here is that the system will call the method **Update** every frame, and no other function. So if you write a method spelt **update**, the system will look for the **Update** function, and since it has not been defined (or overwritten), nothing will happen, unless you specifically call this function. The same would happen for the method **Start**. In both cases, the system will assume that you have created two new functions **update** and **start**.

Best practices

To ensure that your code is easy to understand and that it does not generate countless headaches when trying to modify it, there are a few good practices that you can start applying as your begin with coding; these should save you some time along the line.

Variable naming

- Use meaningful names that you can understand, especially after leaving your code for two weeks.

```
string myName = "Patrick";//GOOD
string b = "Patrick";//NOT SO GOOD
```

- Capitalize words within a name consistently (e.g., camel or Pascal casing).

```
bool testIfTheNameIsCorrect;// GOOD
bool testifthenameiscorrect; // NOT SO GOOD
```

Methods

- Check that all opening brackets have a corresponding closing bracket.
- Indent your code.
- Comment your code as much as possible to explain how it works.
- Use the **Start** method if something just needs to be done once at the start of the game.
- If something needs to be done repeatedly, then the method **Update** might be a better option.

LEVEL ROUNDUP

Summary

In this chapter, we have become familiar with different programming concepts. We also looked into classes, constructors, and member variables. Finally, we created our first script class and experimented instantiating instances and displaying their properties. In the next chapter, we will harness these skills to bring interactivity to our own 3D environment.

Quiz

It is now time to test your knowledge. Please answer the following questions. The answers are available on the next page.

1. A class can have more than two constructors.
2. Different constructors can have the same name.
3. A public variable can be accessed from anywhere in your programme.
4. When a new instance of an object is created, the corresponding constructor is called.
5. All classes created with Unity will inherit from the **Monobehaviour** class by default.
6. The name of a C# script, when created, will be the same for the class defined within this file.
7. So that it can be called from anywhere outside the class, a **getter** needs to be declared as public.
8. In C# the default access type for member variables and methods is **internal**.
9. In **camel casing** the first character of each word is capitalized except for the first word.
10. In **Pascal casing** the first character of each word is capitalized.

Checklist

If you can do the following, then you are ready to go to the next chapter:

- Create a new C# script.
- Attach a script to an object.
- Create a class.
- Create member variables.
- Create member methods.
- Call a constructor.
- Know three of the most common coding mistakes, and how to avoid them.
- Know how to comment your code in a script.
- Answer at least 7 out of 10 of the questions correctly in the quiz.

Challenge 1

Now that you have managed to complete this chapter and that you have improved your skills, let's put these to the test.

- Modify your code to create two additional member methods.
- Instantiate objects and call these methods from these objects.

Challenge 2

In this challenge, you will create your own constructor.

- Modify your code to create one additional constructor.
- Instantiate objects based on this constructor..

3
ADDING INTERACTION WITH C#

In this section we will discover how scripting can be used to add interaction to the game and to provide more control over the game mechanics.

After completing this chapter, you will be able to:

- Detect collisions between the player and other objects.
- Create, apply and detect labels from a script.
- Collect objects upon collision.
- Implement a scoring system to keep track of the number of objects collected.
- Change the current level and load a new scene from the script based on the score.

Resources necessary for this chapter

To complete the activities presented in this book you need to download the startup pack on the companion website; it consists of free resources that you will need to complete your projects, including bonus material that will help you along the way (e.g., cheat sheets, introductory videos, code samples, and much more).

These resources also include the final completed project so that you can see how your project should look like in the end.

Amongst other things, the resources for this book include:

- All the C# scripts used in this book.
- Cheat sheets with tips on how to use Unity.
- 3D characters and animation that you can use in Unity.
- A library of over 40 tutorials (video or text).

To download these resources, please do the following:

- Open the following link: http://learntocreategames.com/books/
- Select this book ("**Unity from Zero to Proficiency - Beginner**").
- On the new page, click on the link labelled "**Book Files**", or scroll down to the bottom of the page.
- In the section called "**Download your Free Resource Pack**", enter your email address and your first name, and click on the button labeled "**Yes, I want to receive my bonus pack**".
- After a few seconds, you should receive a link to your free start-up pack.
- When you receive the link, you can download all the resources to your computer.

CREATING A SIMPLE SCRIPT TO COLLECT OBJECTS

At this stage, we are getting familiar with Unity and creating scripts; to use our skills and to be able to interact with the environment we have created, we will learn how to collect objects upon collision, using some of the built-in functions available in Unity, as well as new variables. The workflow will be as follows; we will:

- Create a simple environment.
- Add boxes.
- Add a tag to these boxes (we will see what this means in a few seconds).
- Use a built-in function that is called when the **First-Person Controller** collides with another object.
- Modify this function so that we detect the label of the object involved in the collision and destroy it accordingly (i.e., collect it).
- Initialize and update the score accordingly.
- Load the next scene based on the score.

So, let's get started:

- Switch back to Unity.
- Select **File | Open Project**.
- Navigate to where the resource pack was downloaded and unzipped, then locate the folder labeled "**unity_beginner_start_project**", select it, and click **Open**.

Once the project is open we can then create our new scene and first script:

- Create a new scene (**File | New Scene**).
- Create a new cube: **Game Object | 3D Object | Cube**.
- Rename this object **ground** (i.e., right-click + **Rename)**.
- Rescale it along the x-, and y-axes **(100, 1, 100)**.
- Set its position to **(0, 0, 0)**.
- Create a new material or use one of the materials available in the Project (e.g., **Assets | Materials** or **Assets | indoor_textures**). You can also look for materials by typing **t:material** in the search field located in the **Project** window.

- Apply it to the object labeled **ground** (i.e., using drag and drop).
- Create another cube; we will be collecting this cube upon collision.
- Rename it **box_to_collect**.
- Place it slightly above the ground using the **Move** tool.
- Add a **First-Person Controller** to the scene from the folder (located in the **Project** window) **Assets | Standard Assets | Characters | FirstPersonCharacter | Prefabs**.
- Apply a red color to this box (e.g., you can create a new red **material** or use some of the materials already available in the **Project** folder: **Assets | Materials**).
- Deactivate the main camera (i.e., the object **Main Camera**). To do so you can select the object in the **Hierarchy** view and, using the **Inspector** window, uncheck the checkbox in the top-left corner.

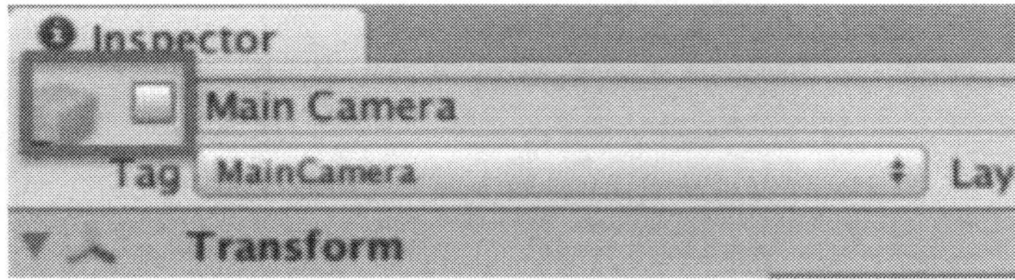

Figure 3-1: Deactivating the main camera

- Check that the **First-Person Controller** is above the ground.
- Play the scene and ensure that you can walk around the scene and collide with the box labeled **box_to_collect**.

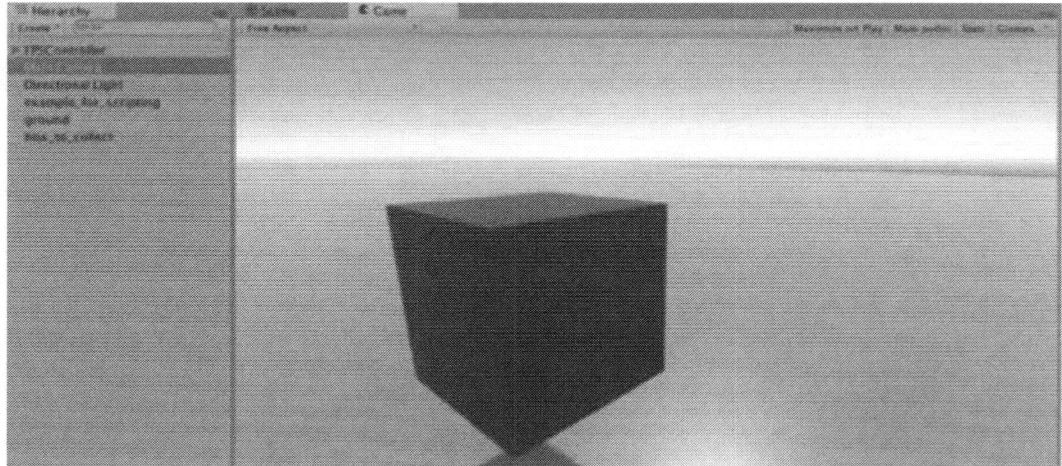

Figure 3-2: Testing your new scene

So far, you have become familiar with the different actions that we have performed. What we will do now is to create a new tag for this object. A **tag** is comparable to a label that we can apply to one or several objects. This helps to categorize objects with similar behaviors. The great thing is that we can check for the value of a tag from a script. So let's create a tag for our box.

- Select the object **box_to_collect** in the **Hierarchy** window.
- In the **Inspector** window, you will notice a section called **Tag** just below the name of the object.

Figure 3-3: Creating a tag

At present, because no tag has been defined or selected for this object, the **Tag** section is set to **Untagged**. So we will create a new tag and allocate it to our object:

- Click on **Untagged**, this will display a list of predefined tags, as well as the option **Add tag...**
- Click on **Add Tag...**; this should display the following window.

Figure 3-4: Creating a new tag

- You may notice that the section **Tags** displays the message **List is Empty**, as we have not defined any new tag yet.
- Click on the + sign to the right of the window (e.g., to the right of the text **List Empty**), as highlighted on the previous figure.

- Then, enter the name of the new tag, **pick_me**, and press return.

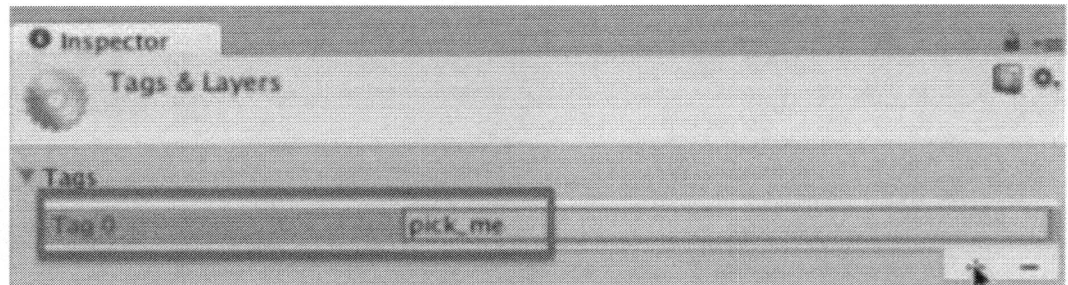

Figure 3-5: Entering the value of the new tag

Now that we have created a new tag, we just need to allocate it to an object:

- In the **Hierarchy** window, select the object **box_to_collect.**
- In the **Inspector**, go to the **Tag** section; you should now see the tag that you have just created in the drop-down list.
- Select this tag (i.e., click on it once), as described on the next figure.

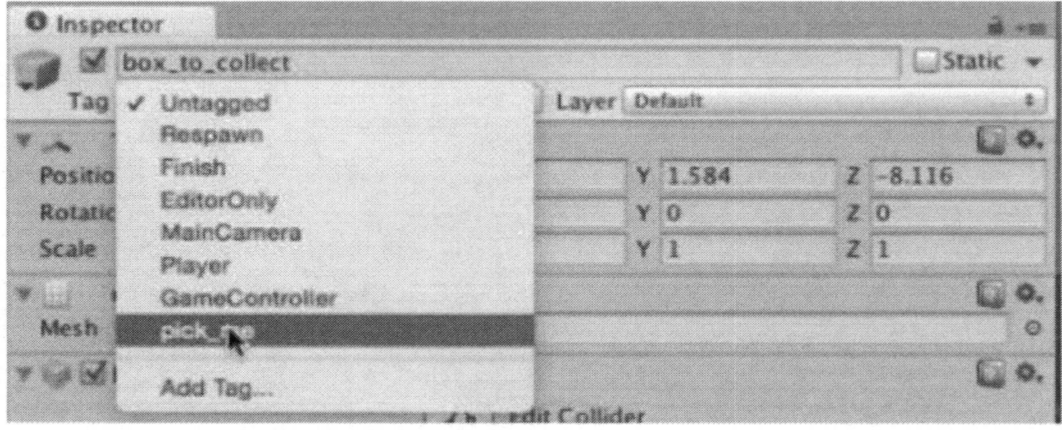

Figure 3-6: Applying a new tag

Now that we know how to create a tag, we can repeat the previous steps to create and apply a tag called **ground** to the object **ground**. This will be used to detect whether we are colliding with the ground. Please select the object called **ground**, and repeat the previous steps to create a tag named **ground** and apply it to the **ground** object.

Figure 3-7: Creating an additional tag for the ground

Figure 3-8: Applying this new tag

At this stage we are ready to create the logic of the game level in a new script that will be called when a collision occurs between the **First-Person Controller** and other objects.

- From the **Project** window, create a new Script (**Create | C# Script**).
- Rename this script **collectObjects.**
- Double-click on this script; this should open the script in your default script editor.
- By default, the script includes the **Start** and **Update** functions.

Here, we will use a built-in function called **OnControllerColliderHit**. This built-in function is called by Unity whenever the **FPSController** collides with another object, on the condition that (1) this function is spelt exactly as Unity expects it, and (2) that the script where this function is written is a component of the object **FPSController** (top-most object). Please add the following code to the script (ensuring that it is created outside any existing function).

```
void OnControllerColliderHit(ControllerColliderHit hit)
{
	print ("Collision with object");
}
```

As you can see, the function will be accessed whenever a collision occurs and it will return information about the collision using the object **hit** (of type **ControllerColliderHit**). The object **hit** will be used to get to know what object we are colliding with.

More information can be obtained on the function **OnControllerColliderHit**, as for all built-in functions in Unity, by using the **Scripting Reference** which is accessible in Unity by selecting: **Help | Scripting Reference**.

In the previous code, the function **OnControllerColliderHit** will print a message in the **Console** window whenever a collision occurs between the **FPSController** and another object. Let's execute the script and test if it works as expected.

- Save the script in the code editor (**File | Save** or *CTRL + S*).
- Switch back to Unity.
- Drag and drop the script **collectObjects** on the object labeled **FPSController**.
- Play the scene.
- You should see the message **"Collision with Object"** displayed several times; this is because you are colliding with the **ground** constantly.
- Stop the scene.
- Switch back to your script.

We will now use the variable **hit** to obtain information on the collision. Please modify the function **OnControllerColliderHit** so that it looks as follows (changes are highlighted in bold):

```
void OnControllerColliderHit(ControllerColliderHit hit)
{
	string label = hit.collider.gameObject.tag;
	print ("collision with "+ label);
}
```

In the code above, we create a new variable of type **String**. This variable is set with the **tag** of the object of the collider involved in the collision. We are using the dot notation, here again, to access information stored in the object **hit** returned by Unity. So again, this object includes attributes that we can gather (e.g., read or write) using the dot notation. Now that we have amended our script, let's see if and how it works:

- Save your script.
- Switch to Unity and test your scene.
- We should now see a message saying "**Collision with ground**" in the **Console** window.
- Move your **FPSController** so that you collide with the box and the console should then display "**Collision with pick_me**".

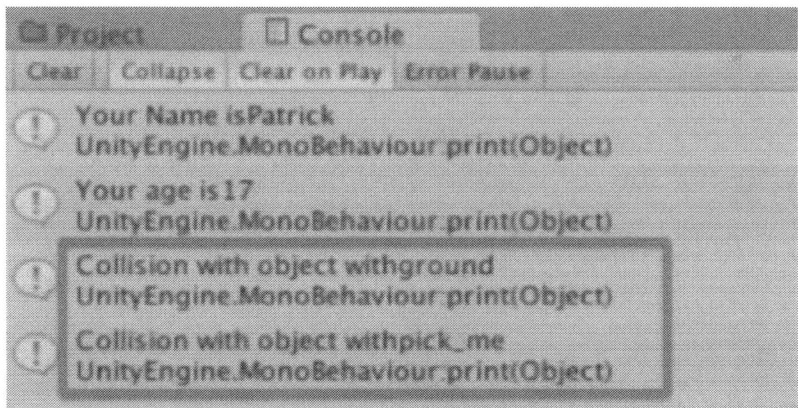

Figure 3-9: Displaying the name of the object we collided with

We will now introduce a new concept: **Destroy**. The idea is that to collect an object (i.e., to make it disappear) we will destroy it. So the idea here will be to destroy the object when we are colliding with it if its label is **pick_me**.

- Switch back to the code editor.
- Modify the function **OnControllerColliderHit** as follows:

```
void OnControllerColliderHit(ControllerColliderHit hit)
{
        if (hit.collider.gameObject.tag == "pick_me")
        {
                string label = hit.collider.gameObject.tag;
                print ("collision with "+ label);
        }
}
```

In the previous code, we check the tag of the object we are colliding with; if this tag is **pick_me**, then we print a message.

- Save this code and test it in Unity.
- As you navigate through the scene, a message should appear in the **Console** window only if you collide with the box.
- Once you have checked this, you can stop the scene and switch back to your code editor.
- To collect the box, we just need to add one more line to the script as follows (the new code is highlighted in bold):

```
void OnControllerColliderHit(ControllerColliderHit hit)
{
        if (hit.collider.gameObject.tag == "pick_me")
        {
                string label = hit.collider.gameObject.tag;
                print ("collision with "+ label);
                Destroy (hit.collider.gameObject);
        }
}
```

- In the previous code, we destroy the object that we have just collided with (i.e., the object linked to the other collider involved in the collision).
- Save this code and test it in Unity.
- You should see that the box disappears from the scene (i.e., in both the **Game** view and the **Hierarchy** view) after colliding with it.

COLLECTING SEVERAL BOXES

Now, that the collection system works, we could duplicate the box labeled **box_to_collect** several times and test the scene to ensure that we can pick-up all the duplicates:

- Switch to Unity.
- Duplicate the box labeled **box_to_collect** three times: Select the object **box_to_collect** in the **Hierarchy** window (or the **Scene**) and press *CTRL + D*.
- In the **Scene** view, move the duplicates apart.
- Play the scene and check that each box disappears upon collision with the player.

ADDING A SCORING SYSTEM

As for many games, it is useful to have a scoring system. So, we could add a scoring system to the game to count the number of boxes collected. Please modify your code as highlighted in the next code snippet (the new code is highlighted in bold).

```
int score;
void Start ()
{
	score = 0;
}

// Update is called once per frame
void Update () {

}

void OnControllerColliderHit(ControllerColliderHit hit)
{
	if (hit.collider.gameObject.tag == "pick_me")
	{
		string label = hit.collider.gameObject.tag;
		print ("collision with "+ label);
		score = score + 1;
		print ("score" + score);
		Destroy (hit.collider.gameObject);
	}
}
```

Once you have made these modifications, you can switch back to Unity, play the scene, and check that after collecting boxes, the score is updated and displayed in the **Console** window.

LOADING A NEW LEVEL BASED ON THE SCORE

The last thing we will do is to change level (scene) whenever we have collected three boxes; to do so, we will create a new scene (a duplicate of the current scene) and load it whenever we have collected enough boxes. First let's duplicate the current scene.

- Save the current scene (**File | Save Scene**) with a name of your choice (e.g., **scene1**).
- In the **Project** window, look for all scenes included in the project, by using the corresponding search field and typing **t:scene**.

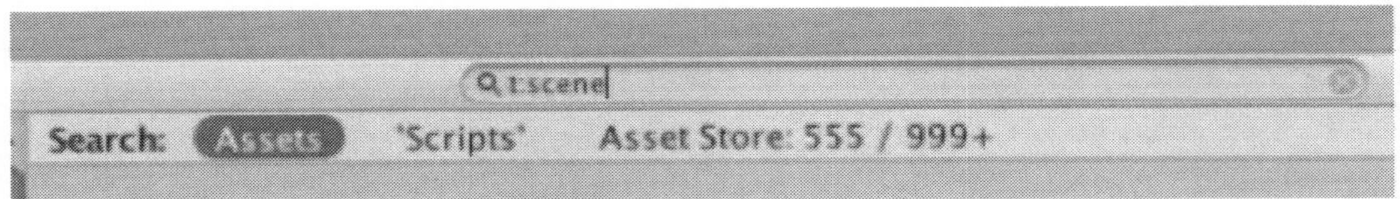

Figure 3-10: Looking for all scenes in the project

- Select your current scene (**scene1**) from the scenes listed in the search result window and duplicate it (*CTRL + D or* **Edit | Duplicate**).
- Rename this new scene **scene2** (i.e. click once on the duplicated scene and select the option **Rename** or press *Enter*).
- Once this is done, double click on this scene to open it (you should see that the name of the current scene has changed at the top of the window, as illustrated on the next figure); I have renamed my duplicate **scene2,** but feel free to use a different name.

Figure 3-11: Checking the name of the scene

- Change the layout of the new scene (i.e., the duplicated scene), so that it looks different from the previous scene and so that you recognize it as your reach it. For example, you can duplicate boxes and move them as described in the next screenshot.

Figure 3-12: Setting a new layout for the additional scene

Once this is done, save your scene (*CTRL + S*), open the previous scene (i.e., the original scene, **scene1**), and switch to your code editor.

At this stage, we just need to check that the score is four or more before we load the new scene (**scene2**). And for this purpose, we will use the built-in function **Application.Load** that loads a scene.

- Open the script **collectObjects**.
- Please modify your code so that it looks like the following (changes are highlighted in bold).

```
using System.Collections;
using System.Collections.Generic;
using UnityEngine;
using UnityEngine.SceneManagement;

public class collectObjects : MonoBehaviour
{

    // Use this for initialization
    int score;
    void Start () {

        score = 0;

    }
    // Update is called once per frame
    void OnControllerColliderHit(ControllerColliderHit hit)
    {
        if (hit.collider.gameObject.tag == "pick_me")
        {
            string label = hit.collider.gameObject.tag;
            print ("collision with "+ label);
            score = score + 1;
            if (score >= 4) SceneManager.LoadScene("scene2");
            print ("score" + score);
            Destroy (hit.collider.gameObject);
        }
    }
```

- In the previous code, we specify that we will load the duplicated scene if the score is 4 or more. Again, I have called my second (i.e., duplicated) scene **scene2;** however, you can change this to the actual name that you have chosen for your second scene.
- Save your code.
- Switch back to Unity.
- At this stage, we are almost ready to go, and we just need to add the current scene to the build settings. By doing so, we tell Unity that during the game we will make reference to and load additional scenes (i.e., in addition to the current scene). So we would typically add all scenes used in our game in the build settings.
- Open the **Build Settings** window (**File | Build Settings**).
- Drag and drop the new scene from the project window to the window labeled **Build Settings**, as described on the next picture.

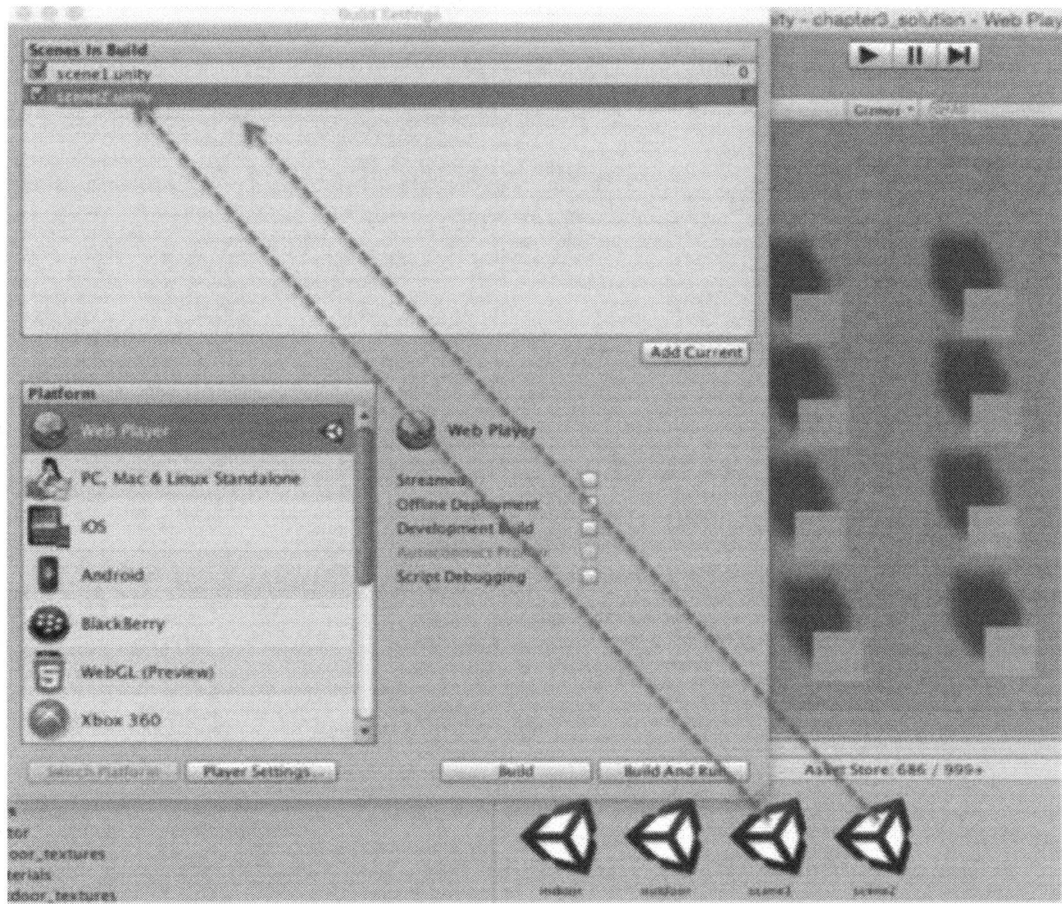

Figure 3-13: Adding a scene to the build settings

- After doing so, the **Build Settings** window should now list, at least, the first and second scenes.

We can now close the **Build Settings** window (by pressing the red button in the top-right corner of this window), and open and play the scene **scene1**; you should be able to collect four boxes and be transferred to the next level (i.e., **scene2**) immediately after.

Level Roundup

In this chapter, we have learned about creating a script using C#. We also became more comfortable with functions, variables, and their properties. We managed to create and use scripts to detect collisions, to collect objects, to increase the score, and to load a different level accordingly. So yes, we have made some considerable progress, and we have by now looked at several programming structures as well as common errors that you may come across on your coding journey.

Checklist

You can consider moving to the next chapter if you can do the following:

- Create and apply tags.
- Use and modify built-in functions.
- Call a function.
- Detect collision between the **FirstPersonController** and other objects.
- Detect a tag.
- Attach a script to an object.
- Destroy an object.
- Understand the difference between the built-in functions **Update** and **Start**.
- Create messages made of static and dynamic information (i.e., append the two).
- Switch between applications using keyboard shortcuts (i.e., not always but at least every second time).
- Launch your game using the keyboard shortcut *CTRL + P*.
- Know the possible cause of at least four common error messages

Quiz

It's now time to check your knowledge with a quiz. So please try to answer the following questions by stating whether the statements are TRUE or FALSE. The solutions are on the next page. Good luck!

1. The function **onControllerColliderHit** is called whenever a collision occurs between the **FirstPersonController** and another object that includes a collider.

2. Given that the object we are colliding with in the next script is named **ground** and that it has been given the tag **pick_me**, the following code will print the message **collided with pick_me** in the **Console** window.

```
void OnControllerColliderHit (ControllerColliderHit hit)
{
        if (hit.collider.tag == "pick_me")
        {
                print ("Collided with"+ hit.collider.name);
        }
}
```

3. Write the missing line in this code to be able to destroy the object we have collided with.

```
void OnControllerColliderHit (ControllerColliderHit hit)
{
<MISSING LINE>
}
```

4. By default, all scenes included in the current project are added to the build settings.

5. Find the error in the following code.

```
void OnControllerColliderHit (ControllerColliderHit hit)
{
        if  (hit.collider.gameObject.tag  =  "pick_me")  print  ("Collided  with  a
box");
}
```

6. Any scene selected in the **Project** window can be duplicated using the shortcut *CTRL + D*.

7. If the scene **scene4** has been added to the build settings, the following code will load it.

```
SceneManager.LoadTheScene("scene4");
```

8. What does this error message most likely mean: **"; missing"**.

   a) You used a variable that has not been declared yet.
   b) You may have forgotten a closing bracket.
   c) A semi-colon was forgotten at the end of a statement.

9. What does this error message most likely mean: **"unknown identifier"**.

a) You used a variable that has not been declared yet.
b) You may have forgotten a closing bracket.
c) A semi-colon was forgotten at the end of a statement.

10. If the **Console** window shows errors and you can't seem to be able to play your scene, what can you do?

a) Check the code using the error message provided (i.e., script name, error line and column).
b) Correct the error.
c) All the above.

Answers to the quiz

1. FALSE (the function here should have an uppercase O instead)
2. FALSE (the code displays the name not the object).
3.

```
void OnControllerColliderHit (ControllerColliderHit hit)
{
        if (hit.collider.tag == "pick_me")
        {
                print ("Collided with"+ hit.collider.name);
                Destroy (hit.collider.gameObject);
        }
}
```

4. FALSE
5. Find the error in the following code.

```
function OnControllerColliderHit (hit : ControllerColliderHit)
{
        if  (hit.collider.gameObject.tag  =  "pick_me")  print  ("Collided  with  a
box");//= should be replaced by ==
}
```

6. TRUE.
7. FALSE (it should be **SceneManager.LoadScene**)
8. c.
9. a.
10. c

Challenge 1

Now that you have managed to complete this chapter and that you have improved your skills, let's put these to the test.

- Open the scripting reference (**Help | Scripting Reference**).
- Look for the keyword **ControllerColliderHit**.
- Identify how the transform property of the colliding object can be determined.
- Use this information to modify your script (**detectCollisions**) and display (in the **Console** window) the **x** position of the object you have just collided with.
- Play the scene, and check that the message is played.

Challenge 2

It is now time to do a little bit of debugging. Not to worry, this will be relatively easy, but it will get you to progressively become more comfortable with finding and fixing bugs.

- Look for a script called **debug_me** in the **Project** window (use the search field or in the folder **Assets | Scripts**).
- Open this script in your code editor.
- You will see that all the code is commented at present (i.e., /* at the start and */ at the end).
- Uncomment the code by removing the code /* and */.
- Create an empty object and rename it **debug_me**, for example.
- Drag and drop the script on this object.
- You will notice that the **Console** window will display error messages.
- The key for you is to refer back to the list of common error messages that we have seen earlier (it is also available in your resource pack, in the folder **cheat_sheets**), and use it to try to solve the errors in this script; there should be five errors in total.
- If for some reason you can't find the error, you can either comment all the code (using // for every line or /* at the start and */ at the end of the script), or delete the script, so that Unity lets you play the scene.

4

CREATING AND UPDATING A USER INTERFACE WITH SCRIPTING

In this section we will discover how to create and update a simple user interface through scripting. Some of the objectives of this section will be to:

- Explain additional concepts on scripting in Unity.
- Explain how to display information from the code to the game's user interface.
- Explain how to load levels and activate objects based on conditions.
- Explain how to display information as part of the user interface.

After completing this chapter, you will be able to:

- Create and display a timer.
- Create a function that displays messages onscreen.
- Modify this function so that the message disappears after a few seconds.
- Display messages when the user has collected items.
- Create functions to maximize your code.
- Use additional built-in functions.
- Activate and deactivate objects from your script.

In this section, we will create a game with the following gameplay:

- The player starts in the maze.
- The player has two minutes to collect three boxes.
- The player needs to collect these three boxes to proceed to the island.
- On the island, the player needs to collect four petrol cans before s/he can use the plane and escape the island.

TIDYING UP THE PROJECT

First, we will create a timer through a script. For this, we will be starting with one of the scenes already present in the project. Before we proceed with the scripting, we will tidy up the scene by grouping all objects already created into one folder, this will make it easy to find and manage the new elements added to the scene:

- Carry-on with the same project that you were working in the previous chapter.
- Open the scene named **indoor** that is located in the **Project** folder **(Assets | Scenes)**.
- Once the scene is open, look at the **Hierarchy** window.
- Create an empty object: select **GameObject | Create Empty**.
- Rename the new object **maze**.
- Select all objects included in the scene except from the one you just created (i.e., **maze**), using *SHIFT + Left-click* or *CTRL + Left-click*.
- Once this is done, drag and drop these objects onto the object called **maze**, as described on the next figure.

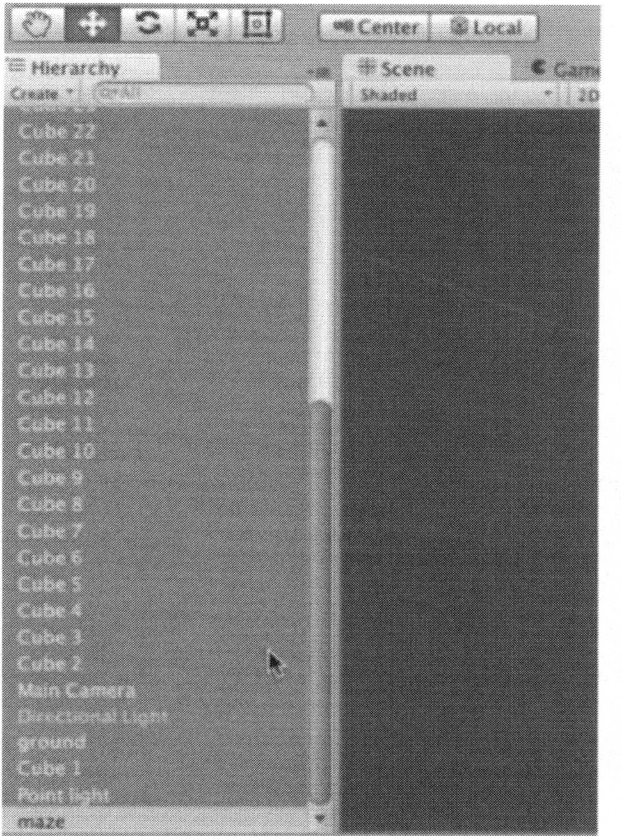

Figure 4-1: Grouping the maze elements - part1

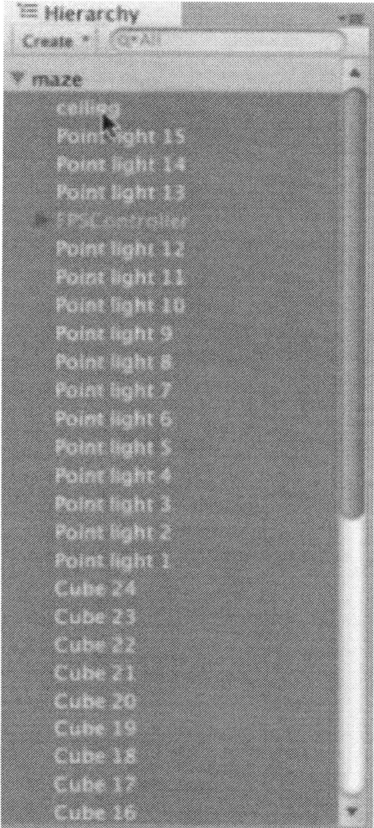

Figure 4-2: Grouping the maze elements - part2

Once this is done, you can see that all the maze elements are now children of the object (or within the folder called) **maze,** as illustrated on the previous figure. This is a nice way to clean up your scene and to group objects.

CREATING A TIMER

To create our timer, we will start by creating a new script:

- In the **Project** window, select the folder where you would like the script to be created (e.g., **Assets | Scripts**) or create a new folder, if necessary.
- From the **Project** window, select: **Create | C# Script**.
- Rename this script **timer**.
- By default, it will include the **Start** and **Update** functions.
- Double click on this script to open it in your script editor.

Once the script is open, we will then create a variable that stores the time.

Please add the following code to the code:

```
float time;
void Start()
{
        time = 0.0f;
}
void Update()
{
        time = time + Time.deltaTime;
        print ("Time:"+time);
}
```

In this example, we create a float variable **time**; we then increment this variable by one every second, using the built-in function **Time.deltaTime**. We could have added just one to this variable every frame (in the **Update** function); however, this corresponds to the frame rate which may vary across computers. So instead, we just use **Time.deltaTime,** which represents the number of seconds elapsed since the last frame. So effectively, the variable is updated every second. For more information on this function, you can look at the Official Scripting Reference. Finally we print the value of the time in the **Console** window.

> So that the time is consistent across computers, it is good practice to use the variable **Time.deltatTime**, so that the actual number of seconds elapsed is used, regardless of the frame rate.

Before we can execute this script, we need to save it and to link it to an object. For the time being, we will create a new empty object and link it to the script; please save your script (*CTRL + S*) and switch back to Unity.

- In Unity, create a new empty object: select **GameObjects | Create Empty**.
- Rename this object **timerObject**.
- In the **Project** window, localize the script that you have just created (i.e., **timer**).
- Drag and drop this script on the object **timerObject**.

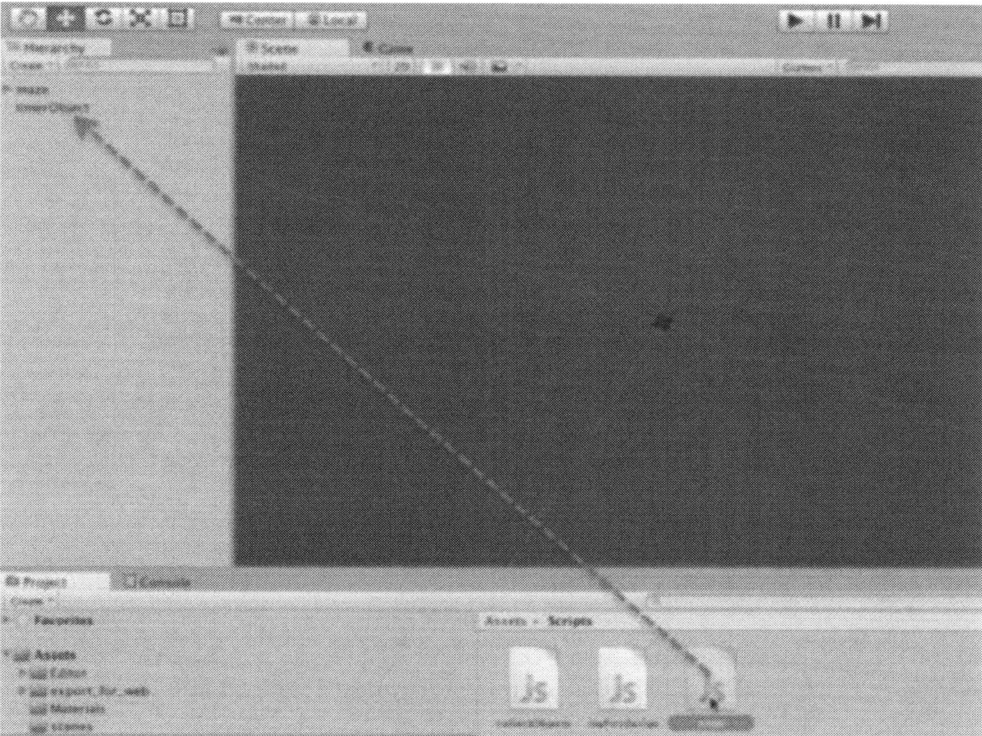

Figure 4-3:Linking the Timer script

- Once this is done, you can check the **Console** window for any error.
- Please fix the errors, if there are any, and play the scene (*CTRL + P*).
- It should display the time.

As you can see the number displayed includes decimals, as the variable **time** used in the script is of type **float**, but we will correct this shortly to display only minutes and seconds.

- Switch back to the code editor.
- Add the following code (highlighted in bold).

```
void Update()
{
        time = time + Time.deltaTime;
        //print ("Time:"+time);
        int seconds = (int) time;
        print ("Time:" + seconds);

}
```

In the previous code, we have created a new **int** variable called **seconds** and we also display it. The difference here, compared to the previous code, is that because we use an integer, the system will not display the decimals. Also note that we convert the variable **time** (which is a float) to the **int** format using the expression **(int)**. This is often called **casting**.

Once you have made these modifications, save your script (*CTRL + S or APPLE + S*), switch back to Unity (*ALT + TAB* or *APPLE+TAB*) and play the scene (*CTRL + P* or *APPLE + P*).

The console window should look as described on the next figure.

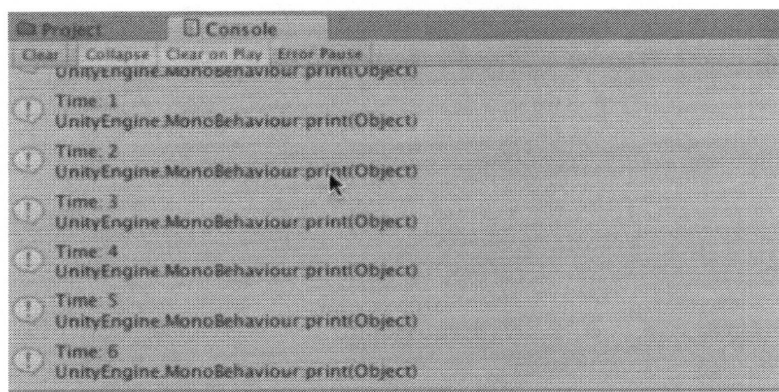

Figure 4-4: Displaying the time

We now need to display the number of minutes following the same format. Please switch back to the code editor and add the code highlighted in bold in the next code snippet.

```
float time;
void Start()
{
      time = 0.0f;
}
void Update()
{
      time = time + Time.deltaTime;
      int seconds = (int) time;
      int minutes = (int) (time/60);
      print (minutes+ " minutes and " + seconds  + " seconds");

}
```

- In the previous code, we create a new variable **minutes**, and we obtain its value by dividing the time by 60 (since there are 60 seconds in a minute). The remainder of the division is not stored yet.
- Again, save your code, switch back to Unity and play the scene.
- The **Console** window should look as follows:

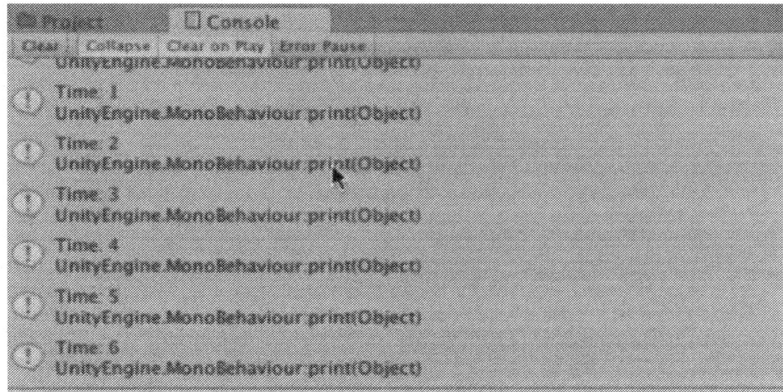

Figure 4-5: Displaying the number of minutes

At this stage, our timer is almost completed; however, there is one issue remaining; that is: when the number of seconds goes beyond 60, it needs to be set back to 0; however, as it is, this number will keep increasing. First let's see how the issue manifests itself, and then we will see how we can correct it:

- Add the following code to the **Start** function.

```
time = 55.0f;
```

- In the previous code, we set the time to 55 seconds so that we can see what happens after one minute has elapsed, without having to wait for 60 seconds.

- Save your code, switch to Unity, and play the scene.
- You should see that whenever the timer goes over one minute, the number of seconds displayed is 61, 62, and so on.

We need to reset the number of seconds to 0 every minute, and we will use the operator modulo **%** that will display the remainder of the division. For example, 62%60 is 2 (or, in other words: 62 = 1*60 + 2).

- Please stop the game.
- Switch to the code editor.
- Add the following code to the **Update** function (the changes are highlighted in bold):

```
void Start()
{
        time = 55.0f;
}
void Update()
{
        time = time + Time.deltaTime;
        int seconds = (int) (time%60);
        int minutes = (int) (time/60);
        print (minutes+ " minutes and " + seconds  + " seconds");

}
```

In the previous code, we have calculated the number of seconds using the operator **%** (modulo). This operator will calculate the remainder of the division. For example, 62%60 is 2 (or, in other words: 62 = 1*60 + 2). So if time is equal to 62, then **time/60** (stored in the variable minutes) **is equal to 1**, and **time%60** (stored in the variable seconds) **is equal to 2**.

Please save your script and switch back to Unity to play the scene. As you do, you should now see that the seconds are displayed properly in the **Console** window once the time goes over 60 seconds.

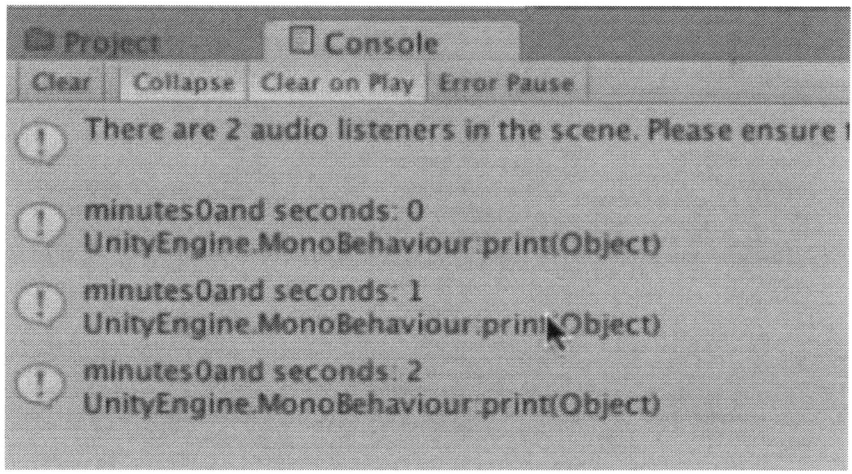

Figure 4-6: Using the % operator

Now that the time is displayed, we just need to tidy up the display of the time by showing only the minutes, followed by a colon, followed by the number of seconds elapsed. This will be handy (and neater) as we display the time as part of the Graphical User Interface (GUI) in the next sections.

Modify the code of the **Update** function as highlighted on the next code snippet (changes noted in bold):

```
void Update()
{
	time = time + Time.deltaTime;
	int seconds = (int) (time%60);
	int minutes = (int) (time/60);
	print (minutes+":"+seconds);
}
```

Save you code, switch to Unity, and play the scene to check that the time is displayed properly.

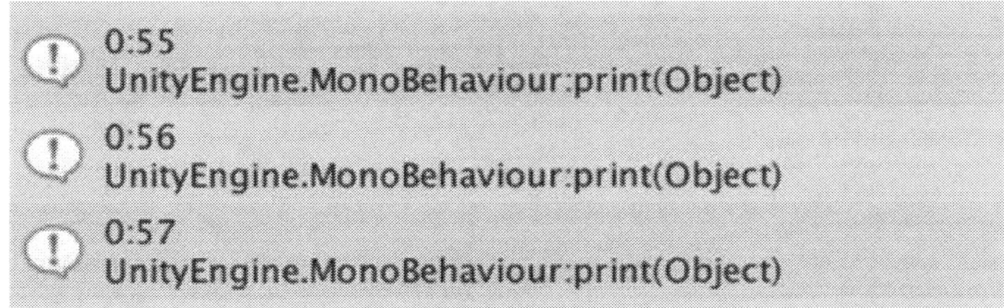

Figure 4-7: Displaying the time in the correct format

As illustrated on the previous figure, the time is now displayed correctly.

Reloading the Level When the Time is Up

At this stage, we have managed to display the time neatly. What we would like to do now is to reload the level when the time is up. To do so, we will check when the time is beyond a certain value, display a message accordingly, and then load a new level.

- Please switch back to the code editor (i.e., the last script)
- Add this code at the beginning of the **class**.

```
using UnityEngine.SceneManagement;
```

- Add this code to the Update function.

```
if (time > 120)
{
        print ("TIME UP");
        SceneManager.LoadScene("indoor");
}
```

In the previous code above, we check that the time is greater than 120 seconds (i.e., 2 minutes). If this is the case, then we print a message in the console window **("TIME UP")** and then we reload the scene labeled **indoor**.

> If you want to make sure that you are using the exact syntax for the name of your level, you can switch back to Unity, open the **Project** window, find the scene that you want to load, click once on it and copy its name, then switch back to the code editor and past the name.

Once you have made these changes, we can switch back to Unity. However, before we can play the scene, we need to check the build settings (**File | Build Settings**) and ensure that the scene to be loaded has been included.

- Open the **Build Settings** window.
- Drag and drop the scene **indoor** from the **Project** window to the **Build Settings** window as described on the next figure.

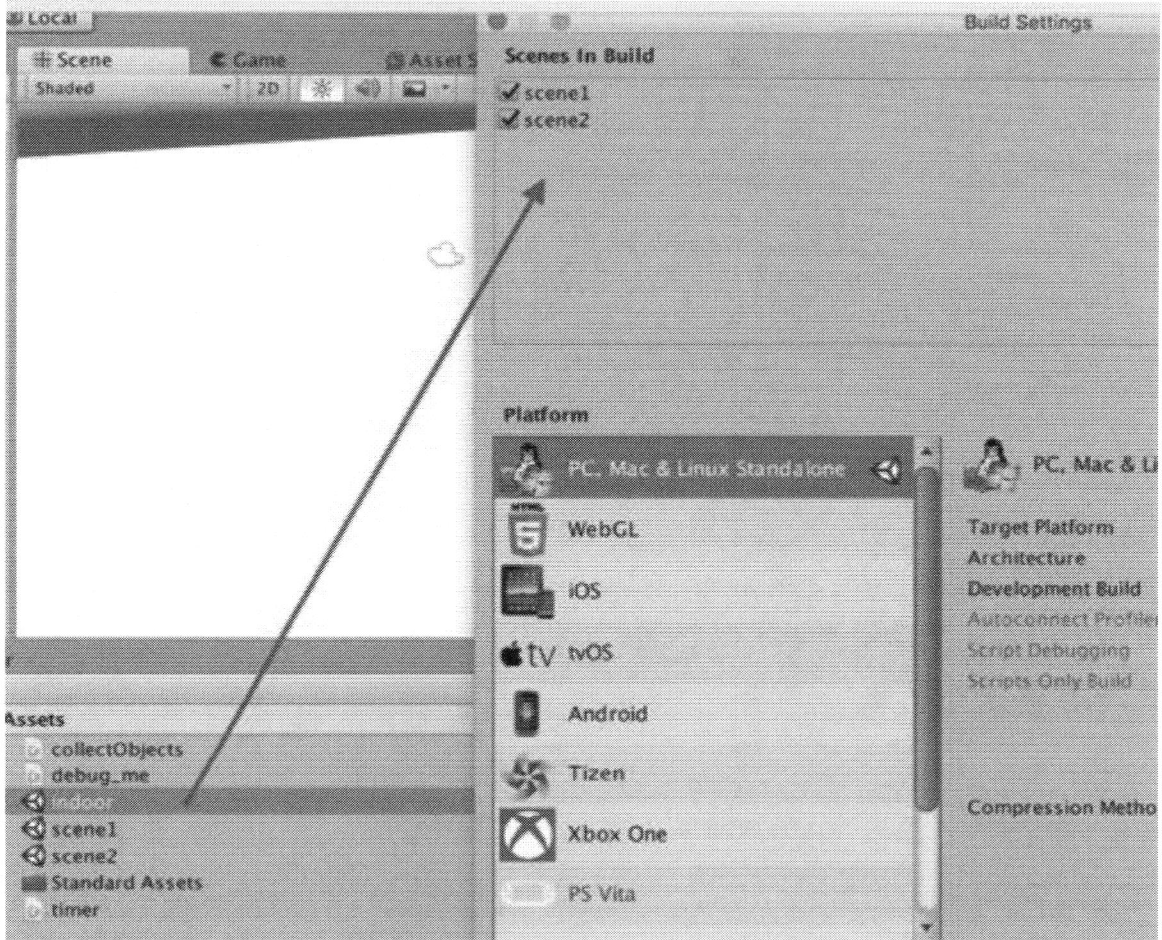

Figure 4-8: Adding the scene to the build settings

Once this is done, we just need to switch back to the text editor and change the initial value for the variable **time** to **100**, so that the time starts at 100 and so that we can see the message straight away (without having to wait for to long). So, please change the following line in the **Start** function:

```
time = 100.0f
```

At this stage, after saving our script and switching to Unity, we can play the scene and see the result of our script. You should see that the time will start at **1:40** to increase up to two minutes. After this threshold, a message should be displayed and the new level should be reloaded.

USING THE USER INTERFACE TO DISPLAY MESSAGES

Now that we have managed to display our message and to reload the level, we will use the user interface for the same purpose so that the user can see messages onscreen.

- Open (or keep using) the **indoor** scene.
- Add a new canvas to the scene by selecting **Game Object | UI | Canvas**. This will act as a container for all other UI elements that we will need for this scene.
- Add a new **Text** element: by selecting **Game Object | UI | Text**.
- If you look at the **Hierarchy** window, you should see an object labeled **Canvas**, and two other elements within: an object labeled **Text** and another object labeled **EventSystem**.

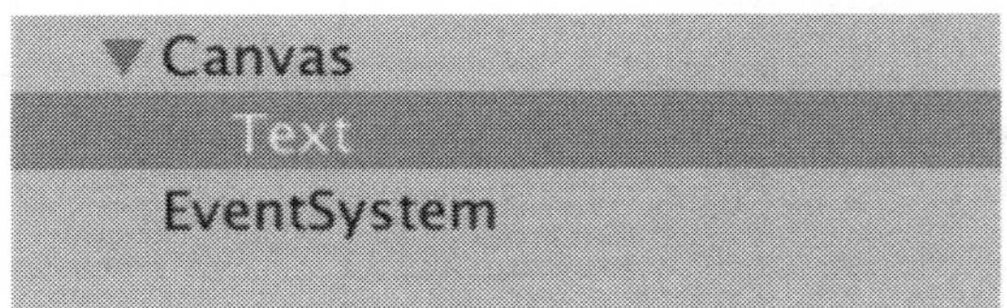

Figure 4-9: Creating a new canvas for the scene

- Because the new element called **Text** will be used to display the time onscreen, we will rename it accordingly to **timerUI** (right-click + **Rename** or single-click and change the name).
- By default, this User Interface (UI) element (**timerUI**) is located in the middle of the screen, so we will move it to the top of the screen so that it does not obstruct the view for the user.
- To work with the UI, you can temporarily activate the 2D mode by clicking on the 2D button, as describe in the next figure.

Figure 4-10: Activating the 2D mode

- You can then zoom-out in the **Scene** view so that you can see the white rectangle that symbolizes the boundary of the UI for the screen (i.e., using the *mouse wheel*) and then focus on the UI component by pressing *SHIFT + F*.

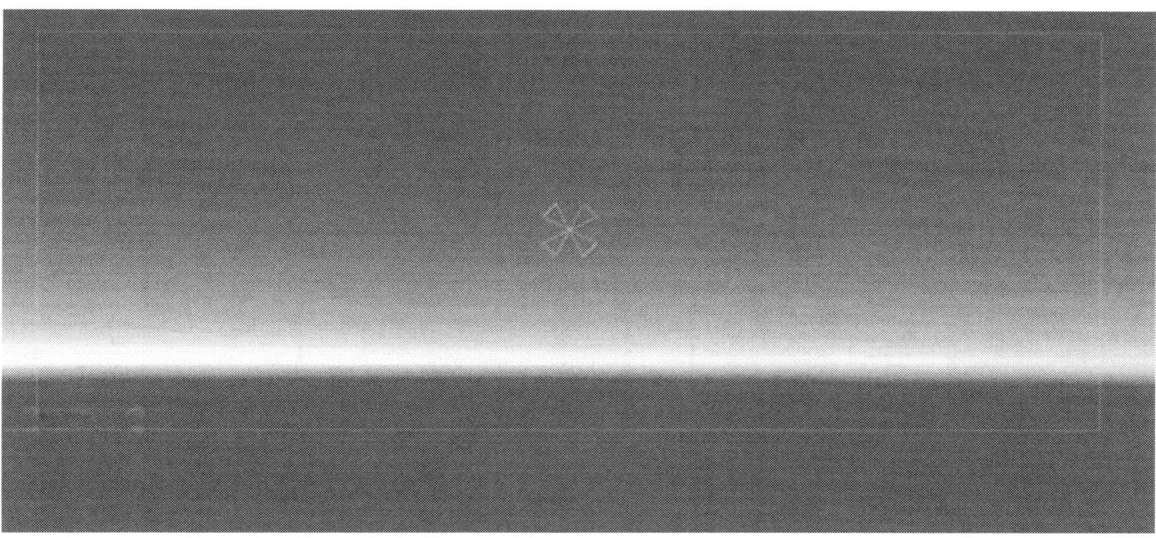

Figure 4-11: Localizing the UI component

- The white outline (i.e., rectangle) represents the area that will be viewed onscreen by the player, so it gives an indication of how the different UI elements will be represented onscreen and their relative position.

- We can now move the object labeled **Text** to the top-left corner by either using the **Move** tool (i.e., the key *W*) and then dragging the green and red handles around the object (i.e., the two arrows illustrated on the previous picture) or the blue square that define the x-y plane (i.e., the blue area highlighted by a white arrow on the previous picture), or by changing the attributes of this object in the **Inspector** window.

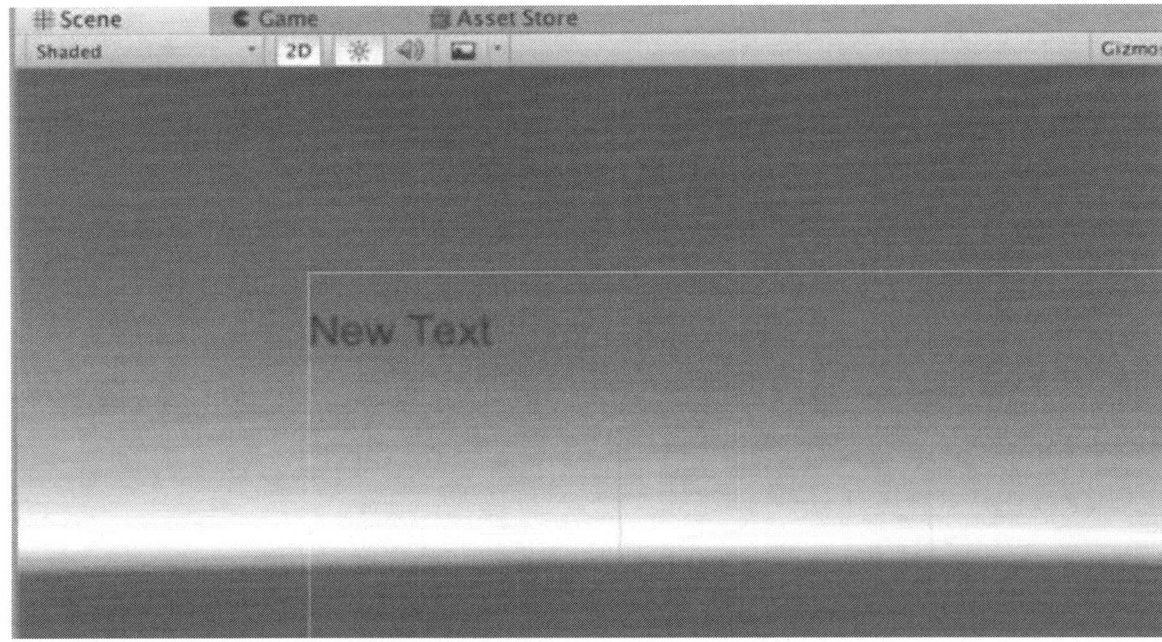

Figure 4-12: Moving the Text UI component

Once this is done, we can change some of the properties of this text, including its **font size** and **color**:

- Select the text object that you have just created.
- Open the **Inspector** window.
- In the **Text** section, change the **Font Size** attribute to **20**.
- In the **Text** section, change the **Color** to white (or any color of your choice).

At this stage we need to access this **UI** element so that messages are displayed on the user interface rather than in the **Console** window.

For this purpose, we will need to find this object from the script and use a new syntax called **GameObject.Find**, which basically looks for an object in your scene, based on its name.

- Please switch to your code editor.
- Open and/or edit the script **timer**.
- Add the following code at the Start of the script.

```
using UnityEngine.UI;
```

- Add the following code to the function **Start**.

```
GameObject.Find("timerUI").GetComponent<Text>().text = "";
```

Using this code, we access the **Text** attribute in the UI component of the object called **timerUI,** and we set this attribute to an empty string. This means that we just clear the text in the **Text UI** for now.

Following this, we need to display the time and to modify our code so that the time is displayed in the UI.

- In the **Update** function, replace the following code

```
print (minutes + ":"+ seconds);
```

with this code:

```
GameObject.Find("timerUI").GetComponent<Text>().text = minutes + ":"+ seconds;
```

- In the previous code, we look for the object **timerUI**, we then access its **Text UI** component; we finally access the **text** attribute and set it so that it displays the number of minutes and seconds.
- You can just comment the code that should not be executed anymore by adding // at the start of the line.
- Save your code and play the scene in Unity.
- You should see the time displayed in the top-left corner of the screen.

Figure 4-13: Displaying the time onscreen

Now that the time is displayed onscreen, we can also create another text object that will display other messages to the user, but this time in the middle of the screen.

- Please stop the scene.

- Select the **Canvas** object in the scene (so that the next UI element is created within this canvas).
- Add a new **Text UI** object to the scene: Select **GameObject | UI | Text**. This text object will be used to display messages to the user.
- Rename this object **userMessageUI**.
- Change its **Font Size** to **20** (using the **Inspector** window). As we will see later, a bigger font (e.g., 40) may not work right now because we need to ensure that the **Text UI** element is wide enough to be able to display text with this font.
- Move the object **userMessageUI** to the middle of the screen.

We will now use code to display user messages onscreen rather than in the console window:

- Please switch back to the code editor.
- Open the script **timer**.
- Add the following line to the **Start** function.

```
GameObject.Find("userMessageUI").GetComponent<Text>().text = "";
```

- As for the previous statements, in the previous code we access the **text** attribute of the **Text UI** component of the object labeled **userMessageUI**, and we change its value to an empty string.
- In the script **timer**, add the following code to the **Update** function (the new code is highlighted in bold) so that a message is displayed a few seconds before the time is up.

```
if (time > 118)
{
	GameObject.Find("userMessageUI").GetComponent<Text>().text = "Time Almost Up.";
}
if (time > 120)
{
	print ("TIME UP");
	SceneManager.LoadScene("week2-indoors");
}
```

Save your script and play the scene. After a few seconds, the message should be displayed as illustrated on the next screenshot.

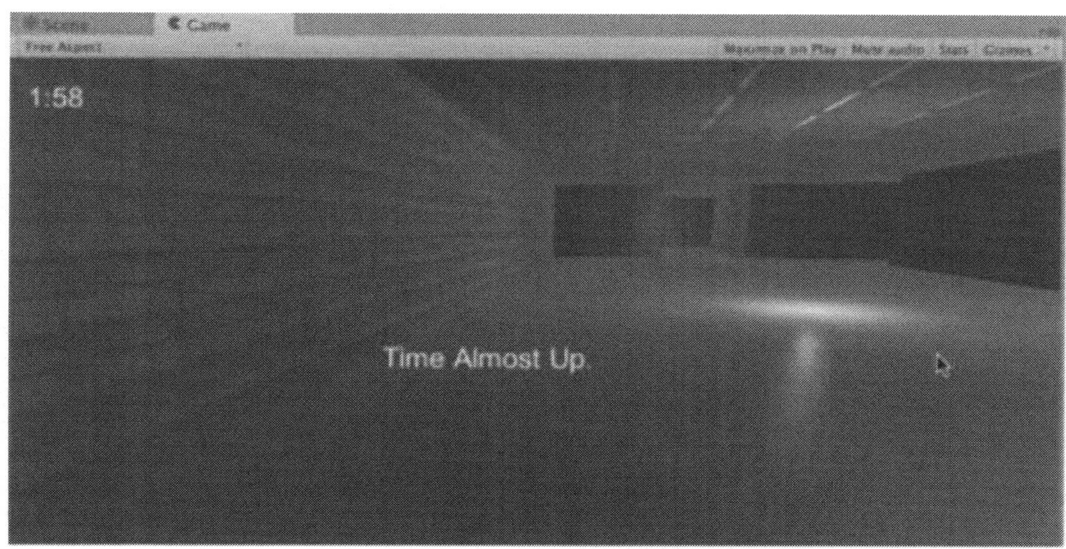

Figure 4-14: Adding a message to the GUI

Collecting Boxes and Displaying Messages Accordingly

At this stage we will add boxes to our level, collect them and display messages accordingly in the GUI.

- In your current scene, move the view close to the **FPSController** (you can select or search for this object in the **Hierarchy** and then press *SHIFT + F*).
- Add three boxes close to the **First-Person Controller** (i.e., **Game Object | 3D Object | Cube**).
- Rename these boxes **cubeToCollect1**, **cubeToCollect2** and **cubeToCollect3**.
- For each of these boxes, you can add a texture or a color of your choice (some textures are available in the resource pack).
- Add the tag **pick_me** to all of these boxes (**Inspector | Tag**)

> You may temporarily disable the **ceiling** object, so that you can see your scene more clearly from above. You can also temporarily set the intensity of the ambient light to **1** (**Window | Lighting**).

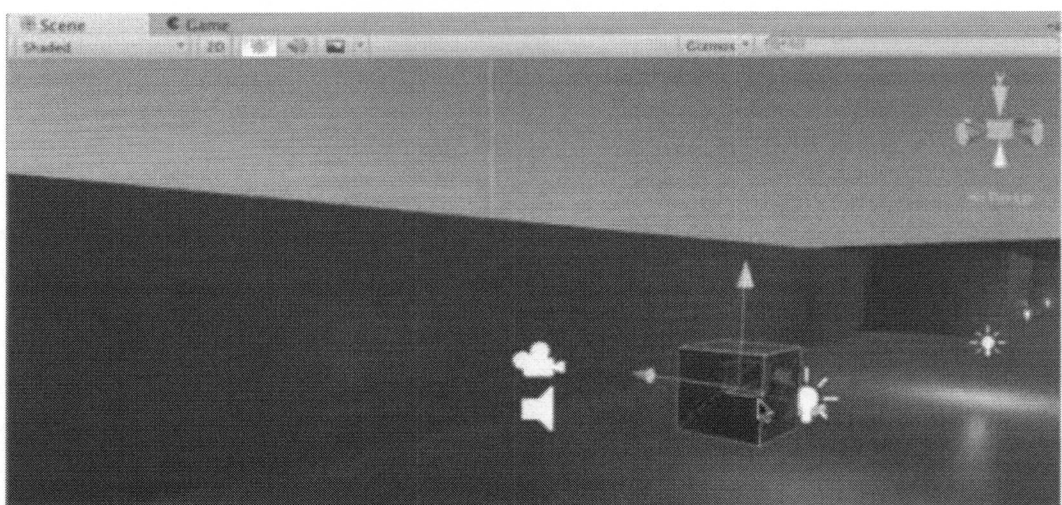

Figure 4-15: Adding a cube to the scene

> To speed-up the process you can create one box, apply a texture and tag to it, and then duplicate this box twice.

At this stage the boxes have been created and we are pretty much ok to go except for the ability to pick-up boxes. If you remember, we created a script to collect boxes in the previous chapter. This script was called **collectObjects,** it detected collision between the **First-Person Controller** and other objects, and it destroyed the objects with the tag **pick_me** upon collision. Because it was created in the same project (although used in a different scene) we will be able to access and reuse this script accordingly.

- In the **Project** window, navigate to the folder **Assets | Scripts** (or the location where you have saved this script previously). You should see a script, among others, called **collectObjects**. If you can't find the script, you can use the search field located in the **Project** window.
- Duplicate this script (**CTRL + D**), and call the duplicate **collectObjects_b** or any other name of your choice (as long as you remember it :-)).
- Open this script and modify the name of the class as follows (new code in bold):

```
using System.Collections;
using System.Collections.Generic;
using UnityEngine;
using UnityEngine.SceneManagement;

public class collectObjects_b : MonoBehaviour {
```

- In the **Hierarchy** window, locate the object labeled **FPSController**.
- Drag and drop the new script (**collectObjects_b**) on this object.
- You can now deactivate the script **collectObjects** from the object **FPSController** by unticking the checkbox to the left of the script, as per the next figure:

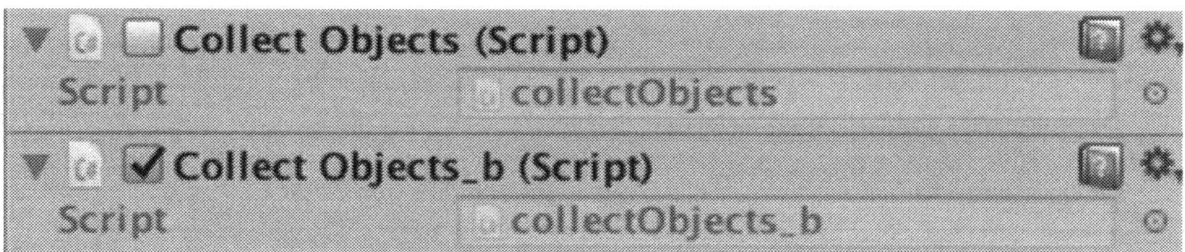

Figure 4-16: Deactivating a script

- Once this is done, the script should now appear as a component of the **FPSController** object, in the **Inspector** window.
- Play the scene and check that you can collect the boxes (no onscreen message should be displayed yet, as we will add this functionality in the next section). You should also notice messages from the new script in the **Console** window that provide information on the score and the object collected.

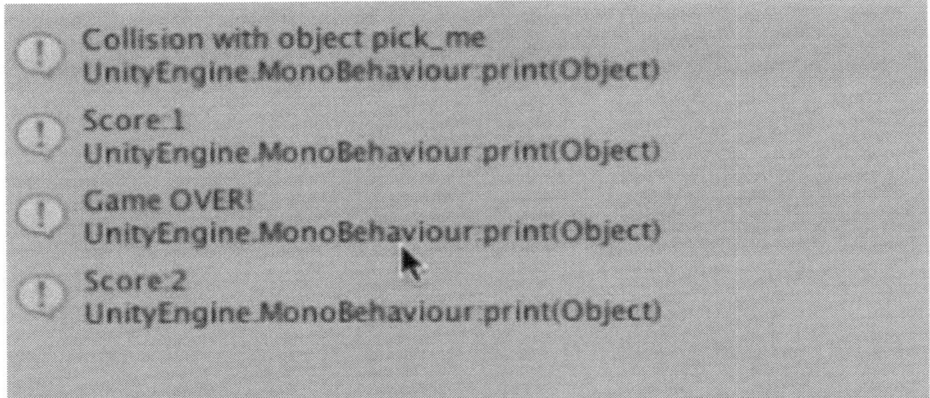

Figure 4-17: Messages from the collision script

If you would like the boxes to glow in the dark, so that they can be seen easily by the player, you can create a new material (i.e., select **Create | Material** from the **Project** window), set its **Shader** property to **Legacy Shaders | Self-Illumin | Diffuse**, and apply this new material to the boxes.

If you can't pick-up the box, it could be due to any of these:

- The labels were not set for the boxes.
- The labels are set but don't match exactly the name defined in the script (e.g., **pick_me**).
- The script was not properly added to the object **FPSController**.

At this stage, it would be great to display more information on the boxes collected. So we will modify our code accordingly.

- Switch to your code editor.
- Edit the script **timer**.
- In the code for the timer, please comment all the code that displays messages in the console window (i.e., the **print** statements).

```
//print ("TIME UP");
```

We will now modify the script called **collectObjects_b** (the script attached to the object **FPSController** and that deals with collisions) and modify it slightly.

Please add the following code at the start of the script.

```
using UnityEngine.UI;
```

Then add the following code (highlighted in bold).

```
void OnControllerColliderHit(ControllerColliderHit hit)
{
        if (hit.collider.gameObject.tag == "pick_me")
        {
                string label = hit.collider.gameObject.tag;
                print ("collision with "+ label);
                score = score + 1;
                if (score >= 4) SceneManager.LoadScene("scene2");
                print ("score" + score);
                Destroy (hit.collider.gameObject);
                GameObject.Find("userMessageUI").GetComponent<Text>().text = "You
collected a box!";
        }
}
```

- In the previous code (in bold), we just display the message **"You collected a box!"** onscreen, through the **Text** component named **userMessageUI**.
- Save your code and play the scene.
- Whenever you collide with an object, a message should be displayed using the **UI** element that we have just created (**userMessageUI**).

However, you may also notice that the message is truncated (i.e., parts of this message are not displayed fully onscreen). This is because the actual text element is not wide enough to display the entire message. So we can adjust this in different ways.

- Please stop the game (*CTRL + P*).
- In Unity, select the object **userMessageUI** and look at its properties in the **Inspector** window.
- In the **RectTransform** section, you may notice attributes called **width** and **height**. Please change the **width** to **400**, the **height** to **200**, and the **Font-Size** to **60**.
- You can also modify the vertical alignment of the text to **middle** (using the **paragraph** section of the **Text** component).
- Play the scene again: the message should now be displayed properly.

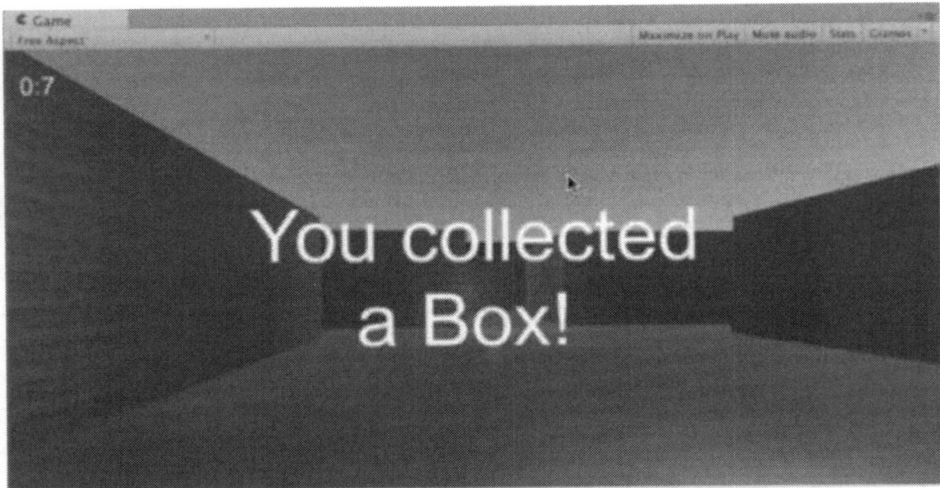

Figure 4-18: Displaying a message after increasing the size of the UI element

So, at this stage we are ok with collecting boxes and we just want to check if we have collected enough boxes to go to the next level. We will make some modifications to our code:

- Switch to the code editor.
- Open the script **collectObjects_b**.
- Replace the following code in the function **OnControllerColliderHit**.

```
if (score >= 4) SceneManager.LoadScene("scene2");
```

- with the following code.

```
if (score >= 4) SceneManager.LoadScene("outdoor");
```

- This will check that if the score is greater or equal to 4, we load the **outdoor** scene.
- Save your code.

As for the previous chapter, because we will try to load a new scene during the game (i.e., **outdoor**), we need to add it to the build settings (if it is not already included), using **File | Build Settings**. To do so, you can either click on the button labeled **Add Current Scene**, or drag and drop the scenes that you would like to include from the **Project** window to the **Build Settings** window.

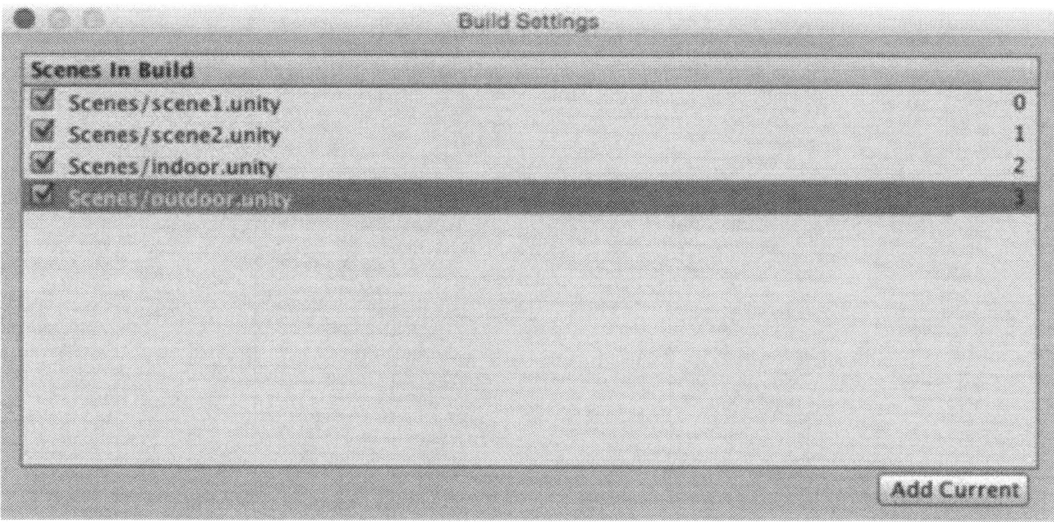

Figure 4-19: Adding the outdoor scene to the build settings

After closing the **Build Settings** window, and playing the scene, we should see that, after collecting four boxes, the player moves on to the outdoor scene. Hurray!

DELETING THE USER MESSAGES AFTER A FEW SECONDS

What would be great now would be to delete the message displayed to the user after a few seconds, so that the screen remains clear afterwards. To do so, we can use another timer to count up to 2 seconds, as well as a Boolean variable to check whether this timer should start. Once the message is displayed, the timer starts; when the timer reaches 2 seconds, the message is cleared, and the timer stops. So let's add these modifications:

- Open the script **collectObjects_b**.
- Add the following code to the beginning of the class new code in bold):

```
public class collectObjects_b : MonoBehaviour {
bool startDeleteMessage;
float timer;
```

- The variable **startDeleteMessage** will be set to **true** whenever we have displayed the message.
- The variable **timer** will be used to count for how long the message has been displayed. Once it reaches **2**, then the variable **startDeleteMessage** will be set to true.
- Add the following code to the **Start** function

```
startDeleteMessage = false;
timer = 0.0f;
```

In this code, the Boolean variable **startDeleteMessage** is set to **false** initially. The variable **timer** is set to **0**.

In the **Update** function, we will check, every frame, whether the variable **startDeleteMessage** is **true**; if this is the case, we will effectively tell the system to wait for two seconds before starting to delete the message currently displayed. Whenever the counter reaches two seconds, the message will be deleted.

- Please modify the **Update** function as described in the next code snippet:

```
void Update ()
{
        if (startDeleteMessage == true)
        {
                timer = timer+Time.deltaTime;
                if (timer >= 2)
                {
        GameObject.Find("userMessageUI").GetComponent< Text>().text = "";
                        timer = 0.0f;
                        startDeleteMessage = false;
                }
        }

}
```

- In the previous code, if the timer has reached **2** seconds, the message is erased, the timer is reset to 0, and the Boolean variable **startDeleteMessage** is set to **false**. This is a simple way to create a timer that will delete our message after a couple of seconds.

- We will also need to specify that the timer (to delete the text) should start as soon as the text has been displayed onscreen. Please modify the code within the function **OnControllerColliderHit** as follows (changes are highlighted in bold).

```
if (hit.collider.gameObject.tag == "pick_me")
        {
                print ("collision with "+ label);
                Destroy (hit.collider.gameObject);
                GameObject.Find("userMessageUI").GetComponent<Text>().text  =  "You
collected a box";
                startDeleteMessage = true;
                score = score + 1;
                print("Score: "+ score);
                //if (score >= 4) SceneManager.LoadScene("scene2");
                if (score >= 4) SceneManager.LoadScene("outdoor");
        }
```

- Save your code and play the scene to see how the code works. You should see that the message displayed (e.g., after picking-up a box) disappears after 2 seconds.

We could now modify this script so that the number of boxes collected is also displayed.

Please switch to the code editor and make the following modifications in the script **collectObjects_b**.

- Remove or comment the following code within the function **OnControllerColloderHit**.

```
GameObject.Find("userMessageUI").GetComponent<Text>().text = "You collected a box!";
```

- Add the following code to the function **OnControllerColliderHit**, after the score is increased, within the conditional statement, as follows (new code highlighted in bold).

```
score = score + 1;
GameObject.Find("userMessageUI").GetComponent<Text>().text = "You collected " +score+ " Boxe(s)!";
```

- As per the previous code, this will display the message "**You collected**" followed by the **score** followed by the text "**Boxes**". So, the sentence includes a combination of static text and dynamic text (i.e., score) that makes it possible to display up-to-date information in a user-friendly way.
- Save your code and play the scene to see how the code works. You should see that the message displayed includes the number of boxes collected.

Figure 4-20: Displaying the number of boxes collected

ROTATING OBJECTS TO BE PICKED-UP

We will now add a mechanism that helps to make the objects to be collected more obvious to the player. We will get them to rotate continuously using a simple script.

- Please stop the scene.
- In the **Project** window, navigate to the folder **Assets | Scripts** (or another folder that you have created for scripts, depending on how you prefer to organize your project).
- Create a new script (**Create | C# Script**).
- Rename this script **rotateBox**.
- Add the following code to the function **Update**.

```
transform.Rotate(0, 10, 0);
```

- This will rotate the object 10 degrees around the **y-axis** every frame. We use the lower case **t** for the word **transform** here, as we will be working with the transform of the object linked to this script. In other words, this transform has already been created and we are modifying it. The **Rotate** function takes three parameters that correspond to the number of degrees by which the rotation should be performed around the x-, y- and z-axes (in our case, the rotation only occurs around the y-axis). For more information on this function, you can look at the scripting reference (**Help | Scripting Reference**).
- We now just need to apply this script to the boxes.
- Select all the boxes to collect in the **Hierarchy** window (for example, by searching for the term **toCollect**) and drag and drop the script from its current location (e.g., **Assets | Scripts**) on to these boxes (or in the **Inspector**), as described on the next figure.

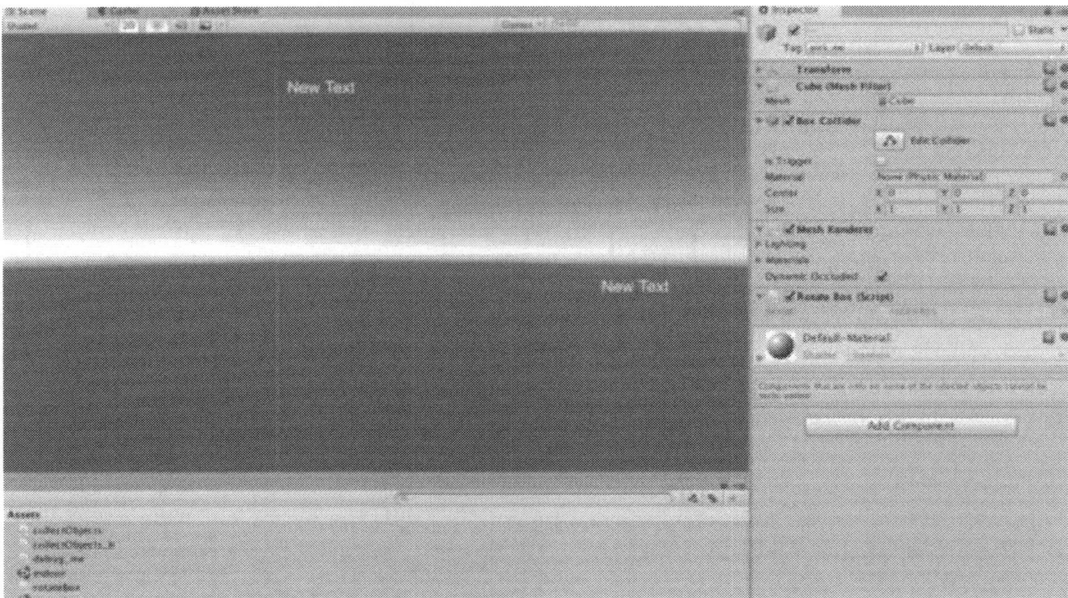

Figure 4-21: Adding the script to several objects

- Check that the script has been added to all the boxes, by selecting each of them and checking that the script appears as a component.
- If you play the scene, you should see that the boxes are rotating automatically. If they are not rotating, please check that the script has been added to all of them.

You can, of course, change the value of the rotation increment to make these boxes rotate slower or faster. We could also change the rotation so that the speed is based on seconds rather than frames. Again this can be done easily, based on what we have learnt so far, and you can change the script accordingly if you wish.

COLLECTING PETROL CANS ON THE ISLAND

At this stage of our game, we have created and managed conditions to transit from the indoor to the outdoor level. We now need to build the logic of the game, so that the player needs to collect three or four petrol cans before s/he can access and pilot the plane to escape the island.

- Save your current scene (**File | Save Scene** or *CTRL + S*).
- Open the **outdoor** scene.

We will now create boxes that will symbolize petrol cans to be collected:

- Create three new boxes.
- Rename them **petrol_can1**, **petrol_can2**, and **petrol_can3**.
- Add a texture or material to these boxes. You can use any texture of your choice or one of the textures provided in the resource pack.
- Create a new tag **petrol-can** and assign it to these boxes.

At this stage we have created and tagged all the petrol cans. We just need to modify our object collection script so that we can detect and collect the cans.

- Open the script used in the previous section (**collectObjects_b**).
- Add the following code to the start of the class.

```
int nbPetrolCansCollected;
```

- Add the following code to the **Start** function.

```
nbPetrolCansCollected = 0;
```

We will then add code to manage collision with the petrol cans. Add the following code to the function **OnControllerColliderHit** (new code in bold).

```
void OnControllerColliderHit(ControllerColliderHit hit)
	{
		if	(hit.collider.gameObject.tag	==	"pick_me"	||
hit.collider.gameObject.tag == "petrol-can")		{
			string label = hit.collider.gameObject.tag;
			if (label == "petrol-can")
			{
				nbPetrolCansCollected = nbPetrolCansCollected + 1;
				print	("Collected	"+	nbPetrolCansCollected	+	"
can(s)");
				Destroy	(hit.collider.gameObject);//collecting	the
can
			}
			print ("collision with "+ label);
```

- In the previous script, we check the label of the object we are colliding with. If it is a petrol can, then the variable **nbPetrolCansCollected** is increased by one, and the corresponding petrol can is destroyed.
- Save this script.
- Then switch to Unity and drag and drop this script from the **Project** window to the **FPSController** object.

Play the scene and check that the cube (i.e., petrol can) is collected and that a message appears in the console window ("**Collected 1 can(s)**").

At this stage, we can collect petrol cans and we would like to activate the aircraft (or make it available) whenever we have collected a sufficient number of petrol cans. So before we modify our script, we will make some amendments to the scene:

- Switch to Unity.
- In the **Hierarchy** window, duplicate the object called **AicraftJet**, this should create another object called **AircraftJet(1)**.
- Activate the object **AircraftJet** using the **Inspector** window.
- Deactivate the object **AircraftJet(1)** for the time being (using the **Inspector** window).
- If you select the object **AircraftJet** and look at the **Inspector** window, you will see that it includes a number of script components. For now, we will not use these scripts, as this object will be used only for its appearance and its collider, so we will deactivate these scripts by unchecking the corresponding boxes, as illustrated on the next screenshot.

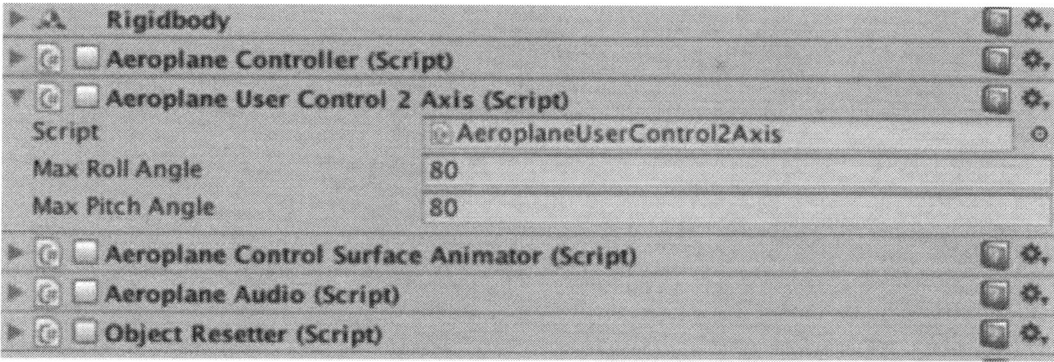

Figure 4-22: Deactivating embedded scripts

Once this is done, we will also deactivate the cameras embedded on this aircraft:

- In the **Hierarchy**, select both the objects **from_plane** and **looking_down** (these are camera embedded on the aircraft, and they will appear as children of this object in the **Hierarchy** window), and deactivate them using the **Inspector** window, as described on the next figure.

Figure 4-23: Deactivating cameras from the plane

- Play the scene. You will notice that you will be able to move around the scene, but that by doing so, while the aircraft is in the scene, it won't move.

- You can now stop the scene.

Next, we need to check that we have collected enough petrol cans before colliding with (and trying to pilot) the aircraft. What we will do is to add a tag to the airplane so that upon collision we can check this tag, and either make it possible to use the plane, if enough cans have been collected, or display a message specifying that more cans need to be collected.

- Switch to Unity.

- Create a new tag called **plane**.

- Assign this tag to the object **AircraftJet**.

As we have seen before, colliders will determine whether a collision occurs between two objects. In the case of the plane, this object is made of several sub-objects with associated colliders, so we will also need to add the tag to the colliders on these objects. To do so, go to the **Hierarchy** window, click on the object called **Aircraft**, then **Colliders**, select all the objects within, and set their tag as **plane**, as illustrated on the next screenshot.

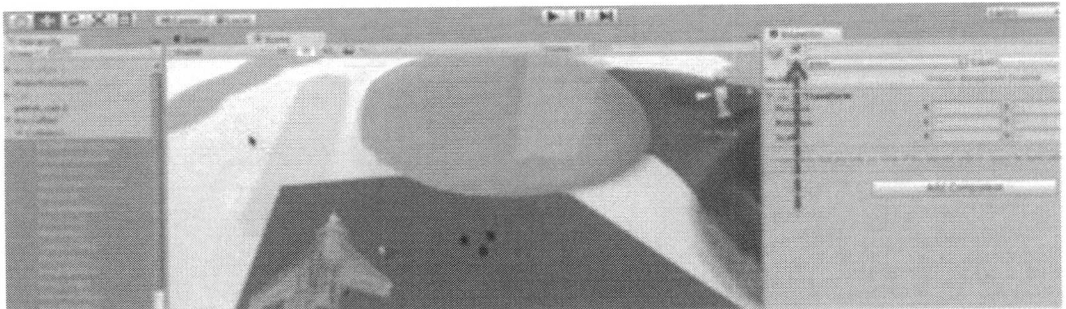

Figure 4-24: Setting a tag for several objects at once

> Note that, instead of selecting all of these colliders, we could have created just one large invisible box collider for the entire airplane; but this would be less precise to check for collisions.

We will now create a **UI** element to display messages to the user; so we will do the same as we have done before, by creating a **Canvas** and a **Text** object:

- Switch back to Unity.
- Create a new **Text UI** object (**Game Object | UI | Text**).
- Rename this **Text** object **userMessageUI**.
- Change its **Font size** to **40**, and its **width** and **height** to **400** and **200,** respectively.
- Change the **Color** of the font to **white**.

As the **UI** has now been created, we can now start to write code to check for the number of cans collected and to also display messages onscreen.

Let's write the code to check for the number of cans:

- Switch to the code editor.
- Open the script called **collectObjects_b**.
- Add the following code at the end of the **Start** function.

```
GameObject.Find("userMessageUI").GetComponent<Text>().text = "";
```

- As you may have guessed, this code just empties the **Text** field at the start of the game.

- Add the following code at the end of the function **OnControllerColliderHit** (new code in bold):

```
if (hit.collider.gameObject.tag == "plane")
{
	if (nbPetrolCansCollected <3)
	{
		GameObject.Find("userMessageUI").GetComponent<Text>().text =
"Sorry you need 3 Cans to fly the Plane";
		startDeleteMessage = true;
	}
}
```

- In the previous code, a message is displayed if the number of cans collected is less than three, and the timer (used to delete this message after 2 seconds) is activated using the Boolean variable **startDeleteMessage**.

- Save your script, switch to Unity and play your scene. As you collide with the Aircraft after collecting less than three cans, a message should be displayed in the **Console** window.

- Switch back to the code editor to edit the script **colletObjects_b**.

- Modify the code related to the collision with the plane in the function **OnControllerCollider** (new code highlighted in bold).

```
if (label == "plane")
{
	if (nbPetrolCansCollected <3)
	{
		GameObject.Find("userMessageUI").GetComponent.<UI.Text>().text =
"Sorry you need 3 Cans to fly the Plane";
		startDeleteMessage = true;
	}
	else
	{
	GameObject.Find("userMessageUI").GetComponent<Text>().text = "Well done,
you can now fly the plane and leave the island";
	startDeleteMessage= true;
	}
}
```

The structure **if/else** means that if the first condition is not fulfilled then the second one will be performed. These actions are mutually exclusive, which means that either the actions included in the **if** statement or the actions included in the **else** statement will be performed: it's one or the other.

Finally, replace the following code (in the script **collectObjects_b**).

```
print ("Collected "+ nbPetrolCansCollected + " can(s)");
```

with this code:

```
GameObject.Find("userMessageUI").GetComponent<Text>().text = "Collected "+
nbPetrolCansCollected + " can(s)";
```

- Save your code.
- Play the scene
- Collect three cans, collide with the Airplane and check that the game displays the right message.

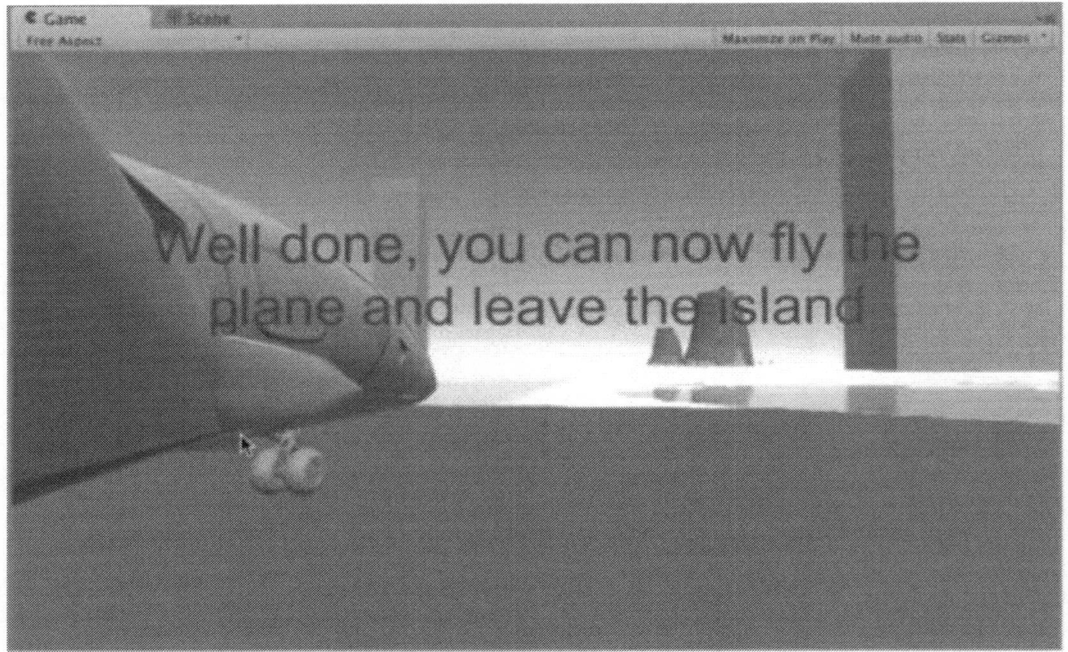

Figure 4-25: Displaying a message after collecting three cans

At this stage, we can collect the cans and detect whether we have enough petrol. We now want to be able to activate the real plane (i.e., the one that has the script necessary to fly the plane) when the player has collected enough cans. If you remember well, we duplicated the jet initially, and we have two versions. An active version is used now to detect collision with the player (no script attached) and the copy that includes the scripts (**AirCraftJet1**) is currently deactivated. This copy is the one that we want the player to use to escape the island, so we will need to activate it at some stage.

- Activate the object **AircraftJet1** (we need to activate it initially to be able to access it later in the script) using the **Inspector**.
- Rename this object **plane**.
- Switch to the code editor for the script **collectObjects_b**.
- Add the following code to the beginning of the class.

```
GameObject plane;
```

- Add the following code to the **Start** function.

```
if (GameObject.Find("plane") != null)
{
        plane = GameObject.Find("plane");
        plane.SetActive(false);
}
```

- In the previous code, we first test whether the object called **plane** exists before trying to access it. This is because this script is used in both the indoor and outdoor levels and because the **plane** object only exists in the second (i.e., **outdoor**) level. So, because trying to access an object that does not exist will produce (i.e., throw) an error, we check for the existence of this object first, before we use it.
- Then we initialize the variable **plane** with the object labeled **plane** (as we have now checked that it exists).
- We then deactivate this object.

Finally, we need to deactivate our **First-Person Controller** after it collides with the plane, so that the player can fly the plane, provided that s/he has collected enough petrol cans. This is necessary, as we want the control keys (e.g., arrow keys), at this stage, to be used only to control the plane. Please add the following code to the script, within the function **OnControllerColliderHit** (the new code is highlighted in bold).

```
if (label == "plane")
{
	if (nbPetrolCansCollected <3)
	{
		GameObject.Find("userMessageUI").GetComponent<Text>().text          =
"Sorry you need 3 Cans to fly the Plane";
		startDeleteMessage = true;
	}
	else
	{
		GameObject.Find("userMessageUI").GetComponent<    Text>().text    =
"Well done, you can now fly the plane and leave the island";
		Destroy(GameObject.Find("AircraftJet"));
		plane.SetActive(true);
		gameObject.SetActive(false);
		startDeleteMessage = true;
	}
}
```

- In the previous code, we first destroy the plane that was just used for collision detection (the one without the controls); we then activate the other plane (the plane we can control), and deactivate the **FPSController**.
- The syntax uses a lower case **g** for the word **gameObject**, which means that we access the game object linked to this script: in our case this is the **FPSControler**.

> To be able to activate or deactivate an object through a script, this object has to be accessed (or referred to) first. This is to create a reference (or a link) to this object that we can then use at a later stage.

The good jet (i.e., the one that includes the scripts so that we can control it) is initially deactivated and will become active only when we have collected enough petrol cans.

- Play the scene, collect the cans and check that you can fly the plane after collecting enough petrol cans. You can control the plane using the keys W (to take off or increase your altitude), S (to lower your altitude), A (to turn left), and D (to turn right).

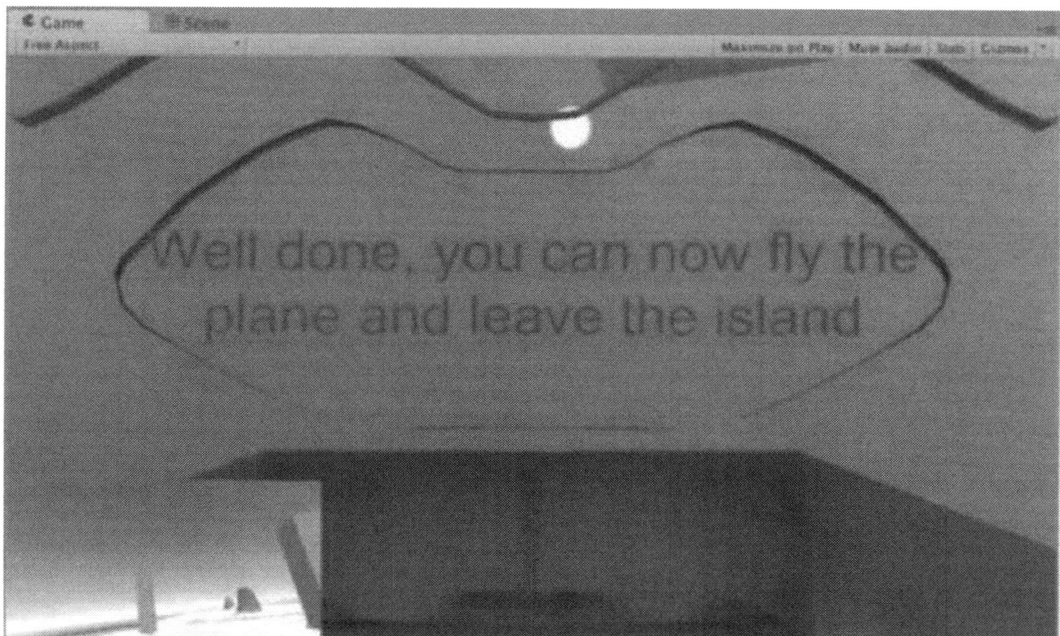

Figure 4-26: Piloting the plane

There is something we could do now to simplify our scripting and make the code easier to maintain (and test).

- Let's switch back to the code.
- If you open the script **collectObjects_b**, you will notice that the following code is used quite a lot, and it would be great if we could find a way not to have to repeat this code.

```
GameObject.Find("userMessageUI").GetComponent<Text>().text =
```

One of the ways to do this would be to create a function that displays a message to the user, that takes the text to display as a parameter, and then accesses the UI element (**UI Text**) and displays the message accordingly onscreen.

- Type the following code at the end of the script **collectObjects_b**.

```
void displayMessageToUser (string messageToDisplay)
{

      GameObject.Find("userMessageUI").GetComponent<Text>().text                    =
messageToDisplay;
      startDeleteMessage = true;

}
```

- In the previous code, we created a function called **displayMessageToUser**. This function takes a parameter of type **string** that will be referred to as **messageToDisplay** within this function.
- The function looks for the object labeled **messageToDisplay**.
- It then sets its **Text** attribute and starts the counter to delete the message after two seconds.

Now that the function has been created, we can modify the code to use it accordingly.

- Please amend the lines of codes starting with the following code.

```
GameObject.Find("userMessageUI").GetComponent<Text>().text =
```

- Replace it with a call to this function using the correct parameter, as described in the next lines.

In the **Update** function, replace the code

```
GameObject.Find("userMessageUI").GetComponent<Text>().text = "";
```

with the following code.

```
displayMessageToUser("");
```

In the **OnControllerColliderHit** function, replace the code

```
GameObject.Find("userMessageUI").GetComponent<Text>().text =
"You collected " +score+ " Boxe(s)!";
```

with the following code.

```
displayMessageToUser("You collected " +score+ " Boxe(s)!");
```

In the **OnControllerColliderHit** function, replace the code

```
GameObject.Find("userMessageUI").GetComponent<Text>().text   =   "Collected   "+
nbPetrolCansCollected + " can(s)";
```

with the following code.

```
displayMessageToUser("Collected "+ nbPetrolCansCollected + " can(s)");
```

In the **OnControllerColliderHit** function, replace the code

```
GameObject.Find("userMessageUI").GetComponent<Text>().text =
" Sorry you need 3 Cans to fly the Plane";
```

with the following code.

```
displayMessageToUser("Sorry you need 3 Cans to fly the Plane");
```

In the **OnControllerColliderHit** function, replace the code

```
GameObject.Find("userMessageUI").GetComponent.<UI.Text>().text =
" Well done, you can now fly the plane and leave the island";
```

with the following code.

```
displayMessageToUser("Well  done,  you  can  now  fly  the  plane  and  leave  the
island");
```

So, this is a good practice, as the function is tested, it can be reused several times.

You can also remove the following code from the script, except from within the function **displayMessageToUser**.

```
startDeleteMessage = true;
```

- Save your script.
- Switch to Unity and check that the console window is error-free.
- Test your game. It should behave as previously, but this time the code is optimized.

LEVEL ROUNDUP

In this chapter, we have further improved our skills to learn about how to create and update a user interface. We became more comfortable with the terms **Canvas** and **Text UI** components. We managed to create scripts to rotate objects, display messages, and to remove messages after a few seconds. We also optimized our code by creating a function that takes parameters and that displays messages to the user accordingly. So, again, we have made considerable progress since the last chapter. Well done!

Checklist

You can consider moving to the next stage if you can do the following:

- Create a **Canvas** and **Text UI**.
- Move the **Text UI** to a particular location onscreen.
- Create a function.
- Use the **Update** function to rotate an object.
- Access a **Text UI** component from a script and update its content.
- Understand how to link to and consequently deactivate an object from the scene using scripting.
- Know where to add scenes to the build settings.

Quiz

Check your knowledge and see if you know whether the following statements are true or false.

1. A new text field can be added to the UI using the menu **GameObject | UI | Text**.
2. The following code will empty the text component named **userMessageUI**.

```
GameObject.Find("userMessageUI").GetComponent<Text>.text ="";
```

3. To be able to deactivate and subsequently reactivate an object named **myObject** from the scene, only the following code is needed:

```
GameObject.Find("myObject").SetActive(false);
GameObject.Find("myObject").SetActive(true);
```

4. Find the error in the following code.

```
void OnControllerColliderHit (ControllerColliderHit hit)
{
    if (hit.collider.tag = "pick_me") print ("Collided with a box");
}
```

5. Any scene can be duplicated using the shortcut *CTRL + F*.
6. If the scene **scene4** has not been added to the build settings, and the following code is used to load it, an error message will be displayed before the scene is played.

```
SceneManager.LoadTheScene("scene4");
```

7. What does this error message most likely mean **"; missing"**.

   a) You have forgotten to declare a variable.
   b) One of the statements in your code is missing a semi-colon.
   c) The function that you have called does not exist.

8. There is only one way to add a scene to the build settings, and this is using the button **Add Current Scene**.
9. If the function **displayMessage** is defined as follows…

```
void displayMessageToUser (string messageToDisplay)
{
    GameObject.Find("userMessageUI").GetComponent<Text>().text =
messageToDisplay;
    startDeleteMessage = true;

}
```

… does the following line of code properly call this function?

```
displayMessage(true);
```

10. The following statements will display the message "**collected box**".

```
bool thisIsTheRightLabel = true;
if (!thisIsTheRightLabel) print ("box not collected yet");
else print ("collected box");
```

Answers to the quiz

1. TRUE
2. FALSE; it should be:

```
GameObject.Find("userMessageUI").GetComponent<Text>().text ="";
```

3. FALSE (the object needs to be declared and linked to at the start of the script also)
4. Find the error in the following code.

```
void OnControllerColliderHit (ControllerColliderHit hit)
{
        if (hit.collider.tag = "pick_me") print ("Collided with a box");
        //= should be replaced by ==
}
```

5. Any scene can be duplicated using the shortcut *CTRL* + *F*.
6. FALSE
7. b
8. FALSE (you can also drag and drop it to the build settings window)
9. FALSE (the parameter required is of type Boolean and should be a string)
10. TRUE

Challenge 1

Now that you have managed to complete this chapter and that you have improved your skills, let's put these to the test.

- Download a font of your choice from the site http://www.dafont.com.
- Unzip the file you have downloaded; this should provide you with a **TTF** file.
- Import this file into Unity (using drag and drop or the menu **Assets**).
- Drag the font file from the project window onto the font attribute of one of the text fields (i.e., **Text | UI**) that you have created earlier. Play the scene and see how the text looks different.
- Experiment with other fonts.

Challenge 2

It is now time to do a little more debugging. Not to worry, this will be relatively easy, but it will get you to get used to find bugs.

- Download the script called debug_me2 from the following link: **http://learntocreategames.com/book_downloads/book2/debug_me2.cs.**
- Look for a script called **debug_me2** in the project window (use the search field).
- Open this script in the code editor.
- You will see that all the code is commented at present (/* at the start and */ at the end).
- Uncomment the code by removing the code /* and */.
- Create an empty object and rename it **debug_me2**, for example.
- Drag and drop the script on this object.
- You will notice that the **Console** window will display error messages.
- The key for you is to refer back to the list of common error messages (i.e., available in your resource pack), and use it to try to solve the errors in this script; there should be five errors in total.

If for some reason you can't find the errors, you can either comment all the code (using // for every line or /* at the start and */ at the end), or delete the script, so that Unity lets you play the scene.

5
POLISHING OUR GAME

In this section, we will finalize the structure and aspect of our game by adding a series of elements that will facilitate user interaction, and that will also improve its appearance; these will include splash-screens, background music, sound effects, and a mini-map.

After completing this chapter, you will be able to:

- Create menus and make it possible for the player to navigate between them.
- Create buttons.
- Manage interaction with buttons.
- Link different scenes using buttons.
- Add background music.
- Mute the music using the keyboard.
- Add and configure a mini-map.
- Display the items collected as part of the user interface.

Creating a Splash-Screen for the Game

We would like to create a splash-screen for the game. To do so we will create a new scene, add buttons to this scene, and ensure that the player, after pressing this button, is transferred to the instruction window, followed by the game (i.e., indoor scene).

- Save the current scene (**File | Save Scene**).
- In the **Project** window, go to the folder **Assets | Scenes**.
- Create a new scene (**File | New Scene**).
- Save this scene as **startingScene** (**File | Save As…**).
- You can save this scene in the folder **Assets | Scenes**.

We can now start to create a button and manage associated events (i.e., click):

- Create a new button (**GameObject | UI | Button**). You will notice that, by default, Unity also created a **Canvas** for this button. The canvas acts as a container for related **UI** components.
- Move the view so that you can see the white rectangle that identifies how the UI elements will appear onscreen (e.g., zoom-out and pan or rotate the view) or temporarily switch to the 2D mode by pressing the corresponding button located at the top of the scene view.

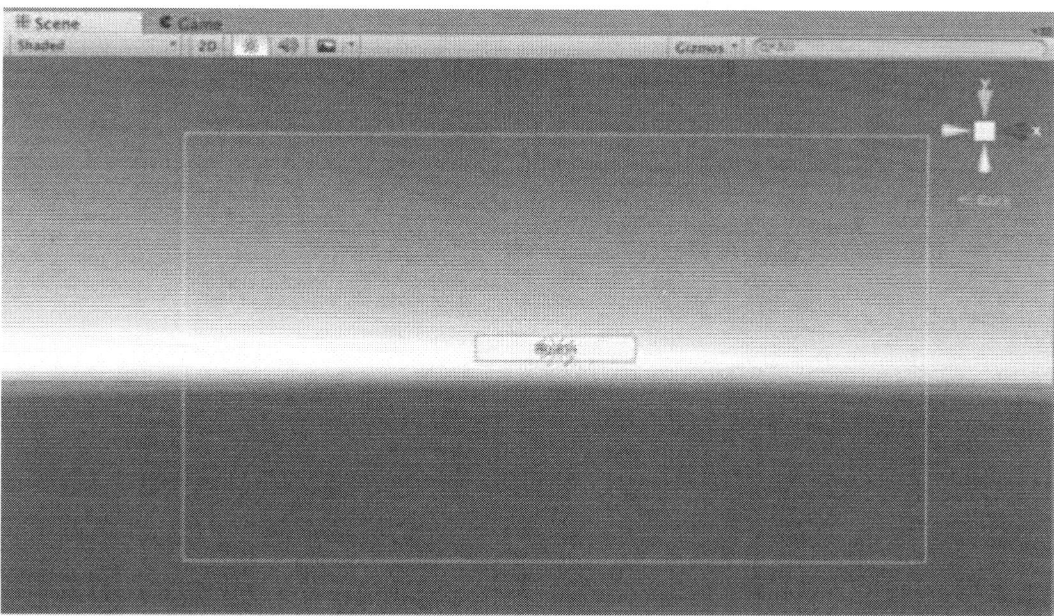

Figure 5-1: Adding a new button

- Select the button and move it to the center of the screen using the **Move** tool *(*the *W* key) and by dragging it along the **x-** (red) or **y-axis** (green).
- We can now change the color of this button: select the button and, using the **Inspector** window, change its attribute **Normal Color**, in the component labeled **Button**, to a color of your choice.

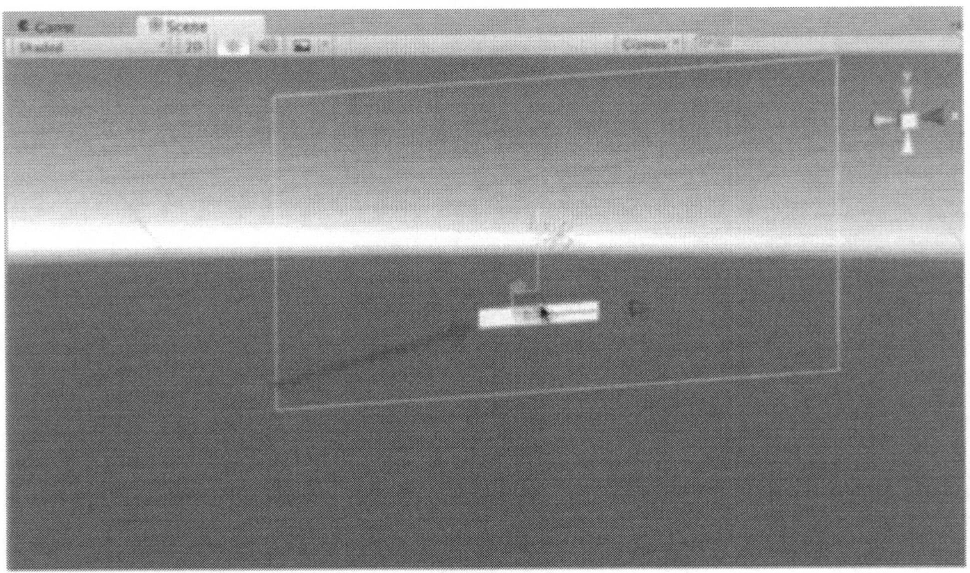

Figure 5-2: Moving the new button

For an interaction to be created (i.e., to detect a click on this button), we will need to create a script. This script will include a function that will be called whenever the button is clicked.

- Create a new script: in the **Project** window, select **Create | C# Script**.
- Rename this script **manageMenu** (i.e., click once on the name of the script or select the script and press *Enter*).
- Open the script in your code editor (i.e., double click on the script).
- Add the following code at the beginning of the class.

```
using UnityEngine.SceneManagement;
```

- Create a new function called **loadMainGame** by adding the following code to the script.

```
public void loadMainGame()
{
      SceneManager.LoadScene("indoor");
}
```

- When called, this function will load the **indoor** scene. If you have named your indoor scene differently, then you will also need to amend the script accordingly (e.g., change the word "**indoor**" to the name that you have given to your indoor scene).

We now need to link the script to the button.

There are several ways to achieve this, and one of them is to proceed as follows:

- Switch to Unity.
- Create an empty object (**GameObject | Create Empty**).
- Rename this object **containsScript**, as it will be used to store scripts to be used for interactions with buttons.
- Drag and drop the script **manageMenu** from the Project window to this empty object.

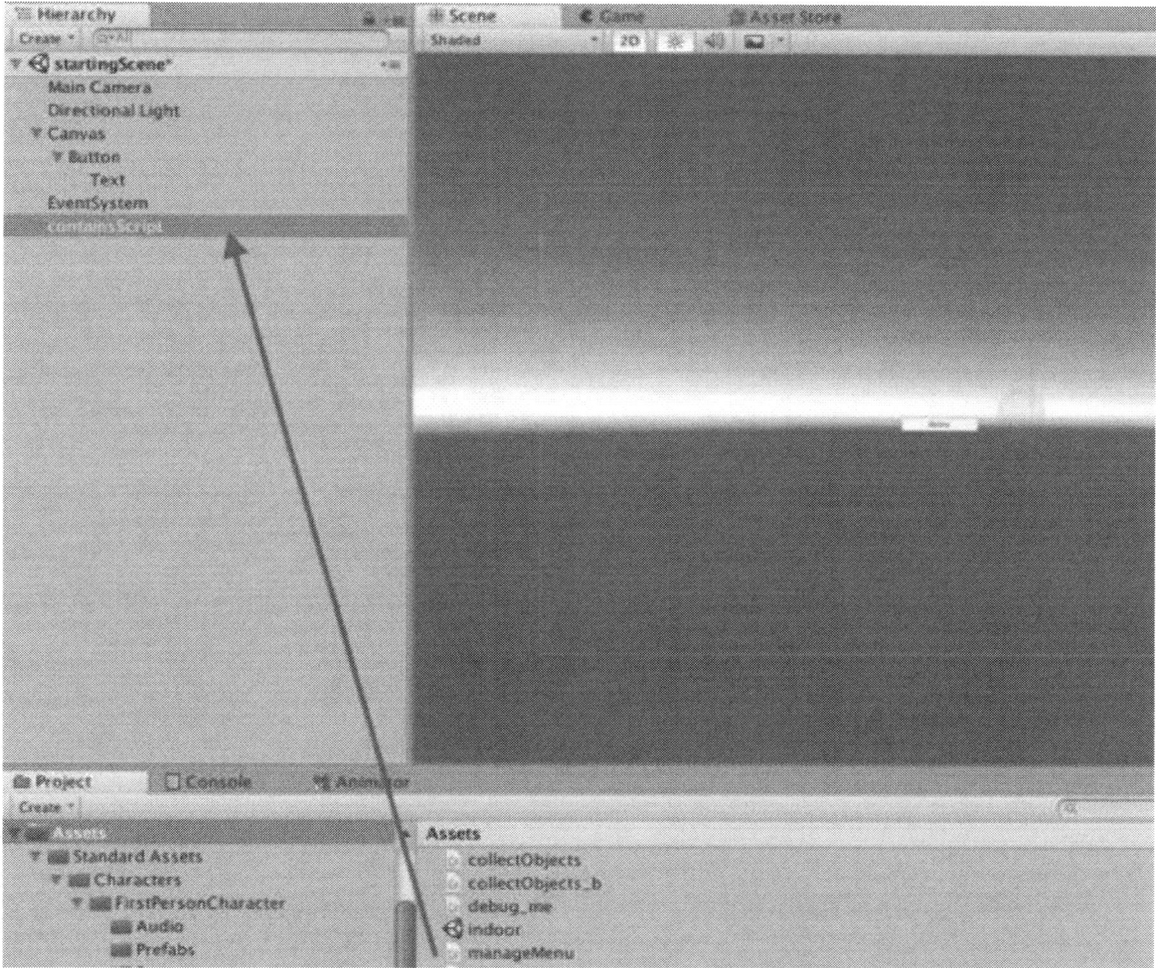

Figure 5-3: Adding the script

- In the **Hierarchy,** select the button that you have created.
- Look at the properties of this object in the **Inspector** window, scroll down, and click on the + sign located in the section labeled **OnClick()**, within the component called **Button**. This should display a new section, in the **Inspector**, that can be used to specify what will be done when a click is performed on the button, as described in the next figure.

Figure 5-4: Managing clicks

- As you can see, it consists of an empty placeholder **labeled None (Object)**, where an object should be added. So we will drag and drop the object **containsScript** into this container, as illustrated on the next screenshot.

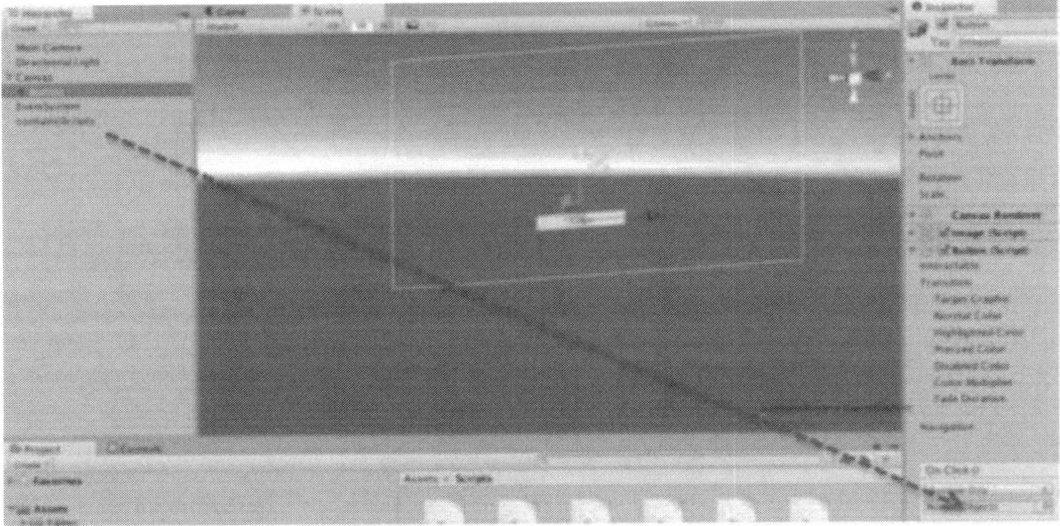

Figure 5-5: Attaching the "script container" to the button

- If you click on the drop down menu to the right of the menu labeled **No function**, you will now see all the scripts and functions contained in the object we have just dropped (i.e., **containsScript**). In other words, we can now, in case the user clicks on the button, access any of these scripts and call corresponding functions.

We will now select the script and function that should be called:

- Click on the label **No Function**.
- Select **manageMenu | loadMainGame**, as described on the next figure.

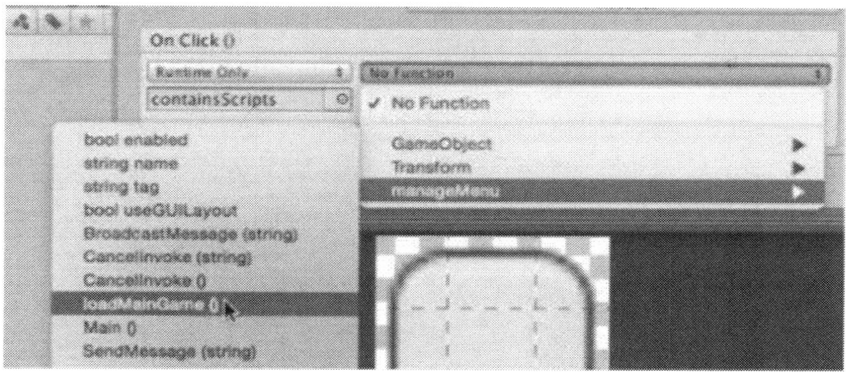

Figure 5-6: Linking the script to the button

- So again, by now, if we click on the button, the function **loadMainGame** should be called, which means that the first level (**indoor** scene) will be loaded.
- Play the scene, and check that it works properly by clicking on the button (i.e., check that the **indoor** scene loads after pressing the button).

> If the indoor scene is too dark, go to the menu Window | Lighting | Settings. You can then select the tab called **Scene**, navigate to the section called **Lightmapping Settings** and uncheck the box called **Auto Generate**.

So, as we have created the splash-screen, we could now create another scene for the end of the game.

- Save the current scene (*CTRL + S*).
- Create a new scene (**File | New Scene**).
- Save it as **theEnd** (**File | Save As**).

We will now create a new user interface for this scene.

- Create a new text object: **GameObject | UI | Text** (it will automatically create the corresponding canvas).
- In the **Hierarchy** view, select the **Text** object that has just been created.

Open the **Inspector** window, and change the attributes of this object as follows (as illustrated on the next figure):

- **Text**: **Well done! You have managed to escape the island**.
- **Width**: **600** (in the **Rect Transform** section).

- **Height**: **200** (in the **Rect Transform** section).
- **Paragraph alignment**: **centre align**.
- **Font-Size**: **40**.

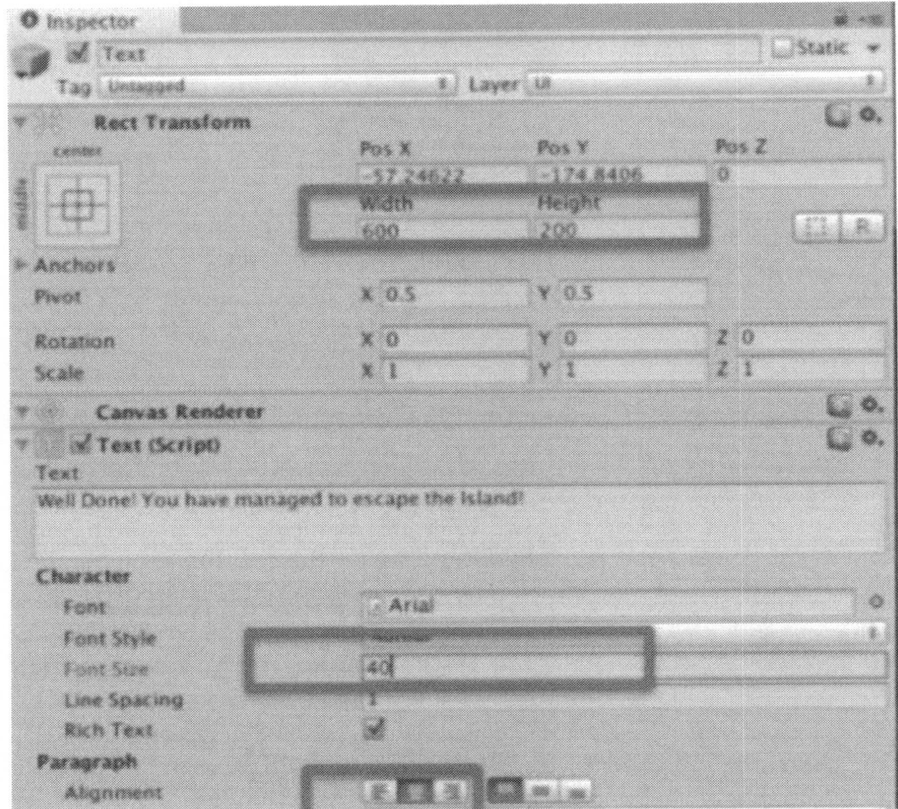

Figure 5-7: Changing the properties of the Text object

- We can also move the text object to the center of the screen, by using the **Move** tool and dragging the object along the **x-** and **z-axes**.
- You can also change the color of the text if you wish.

We can now add a button to this scene; this button will be used to restart the game.

- Create a new button (**GameObject | UI | Button**). You will notice that, by default, Unity will add this button to the existing canvas.
- Pan the view so that you can see the white rectangle that identifies how the UI elements will appear onscreen.
- Select the button and move it just below the previous text.

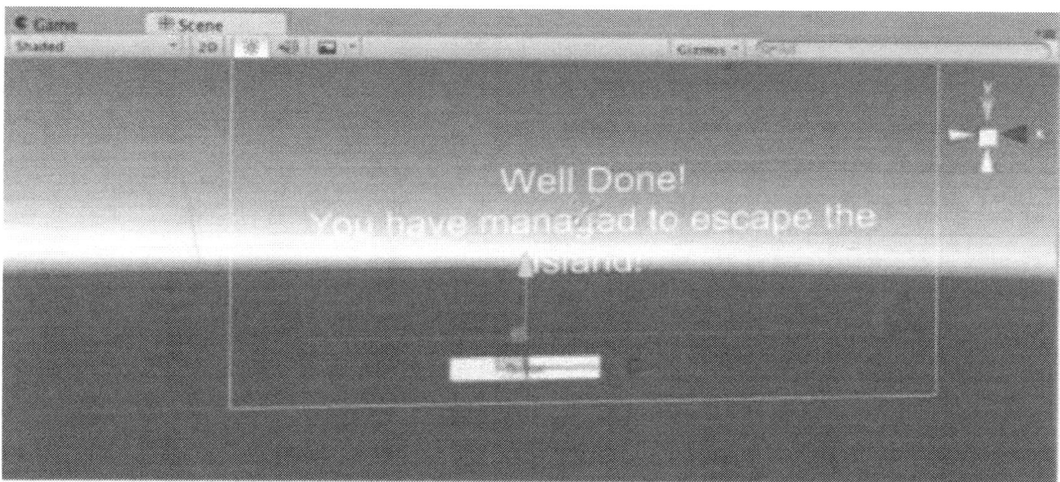

Figure 5-8: Moving the button below the text

As we have created the button, we will need to determine what script will be called when the user clicks on it. As for the previous scene, we will need to create an empty object that contains the script and function to be called.

- Create an empty object (**GameObject | Create Empty**).
- Rename this object **containsScript**, as it will be used to store scripts to be used for interactions with buttons.
- Drag and drop the script **manageMenu** to this empty object.

The script will need to be modified slightly, because at this stage (end scene) we need a new function that will reload the first level (i.e., the splash-screen).

- Open the script **manageMenu** and add the following code to the end of the script.

```
public void restartGame()
{
	SceneManager.LoadScene("startingScene");
}
```

- This function will load the splash-screen scene, provided that you called it **startingScene**.
- Save your code and check, using the **Build Settings** window (**File | Build Settings**), that this scene is included to the build.
- We can add both the splash-screen (the scene **startingScene**) and the end scene (the scene **theEnd**) to the **Build Settings** window, by dragging and dropping them from the folder **Assets | Scenes** (or another location where you have saved these scenes) to the **Build Settings** window.

> If you can't find where you have saved your scenes, you can search for them by using the search field in the **Project** window and by using the keyword **t:scene**. This will list all scenes in the current project.

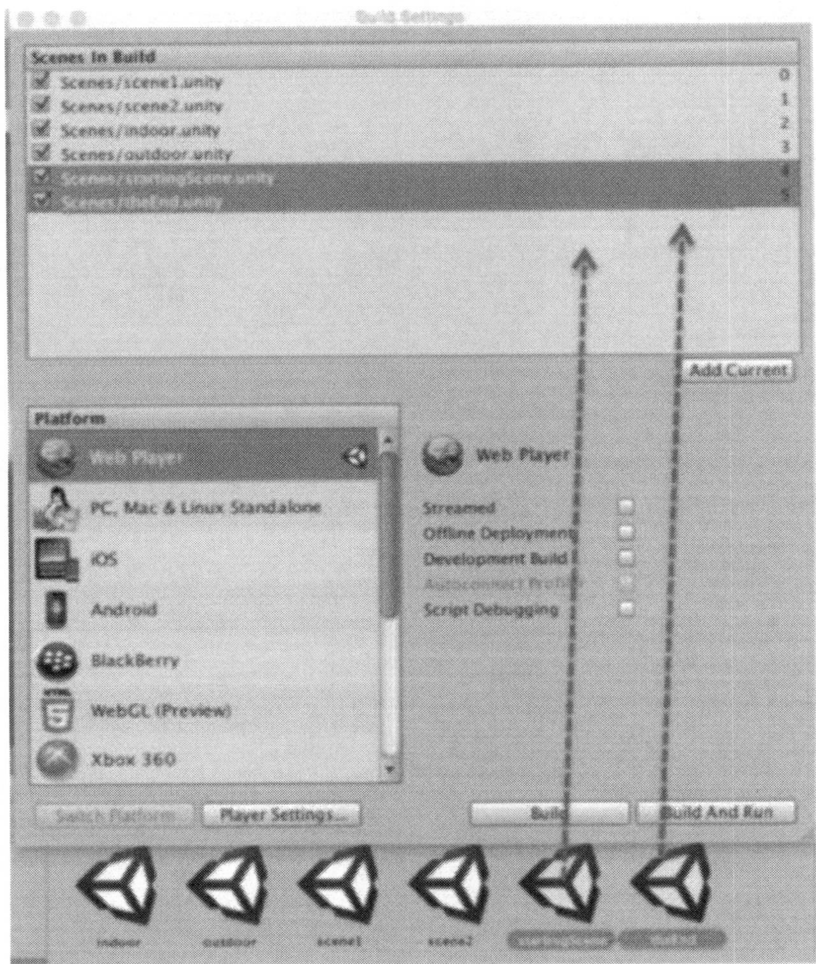

Figure 5-9: Adding the start and end scenes to the build settings

- Once this is done, you can close this window.

By now, we just need to link the script to the button, as we have done previously.

- Select the button in the **Hierarchy**.
- Look at the properties of this object in the **Inspector** window, and click on the + sign located in the section labeled **OnClick()**, within the component called **Button**. This displays a new section in the **Inspector** that can be used to specify what will be done when a click is performed on the button.

- Drag and drop the object **containsScript** to the empty placeholder, as we have done for the previous scene.
- Click on the label **No Function**.
- Select **manageMenu | restartGame**.

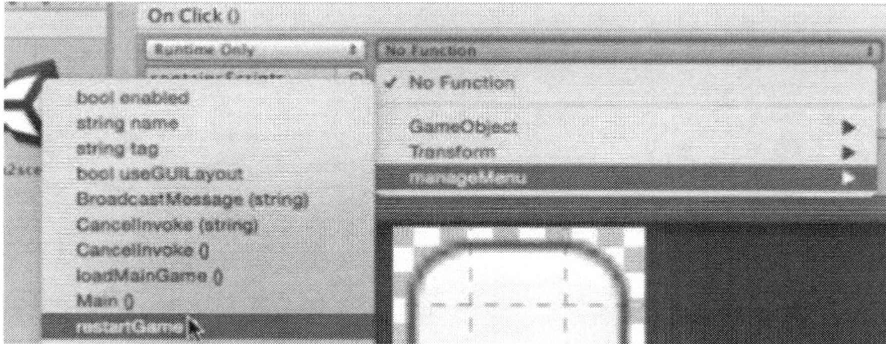

Figure 5-10: Linking the script to the button

- Again, here we linked the script and the function **restartGame** to this button.
- Test the scene, and as you click on the button, you should be transferred back to the first scene (i.e., **startingScene**).

We will now start to tidy-up the splash-screen and other screens also.

First we will change the labels of the buttons.

- In the current scene (i.e., the scene **theEnd**), select the **Text** object that is within (i.e., is a child of) the button, as illustrated in the next figure.

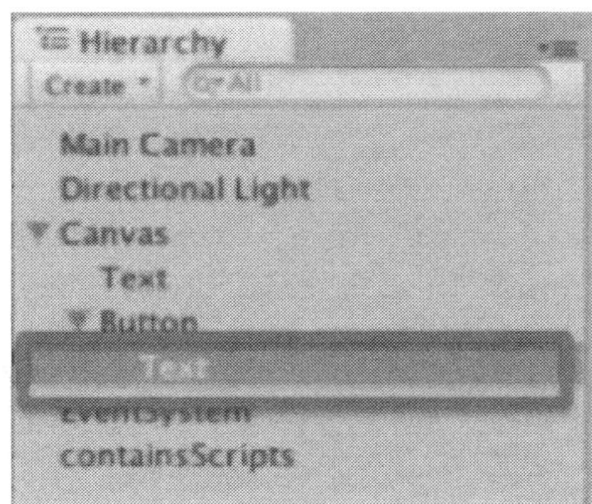

Figure 5-11: Selecting the text label for the button

- This object includes information about how the label of the button will look like.
- In the **Inspector**, change the **text** attribute of this object to >> **Click to Restart** <<.

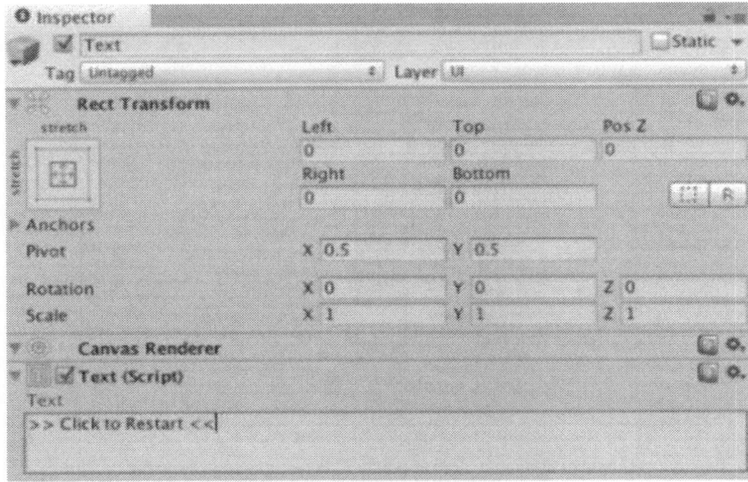

Figure 5-12: Modifying the label of the button

- Save your scene (**File | Save Scene**).

We will now modify the **splash-screen**, using the same principle. First, we will add instructions for the game:

- Open the splash-screen scene (i.e., the scene **startingScene**).
- Add a **Text UI** object (**GameObject | UI | Text**) to the scene.

Change its text attributes as follows:

- **Text**: **Collect Four Boxes before the time is up and then collect all petrol cans and escape the island**
- **Width**: **600**
- **Height**: **200**
- **Font-size**: **40**
- **Color**: **White**
- **Alignment**: **Centre**

Move this text object in the **Scene** view, so that it appears just above the button.

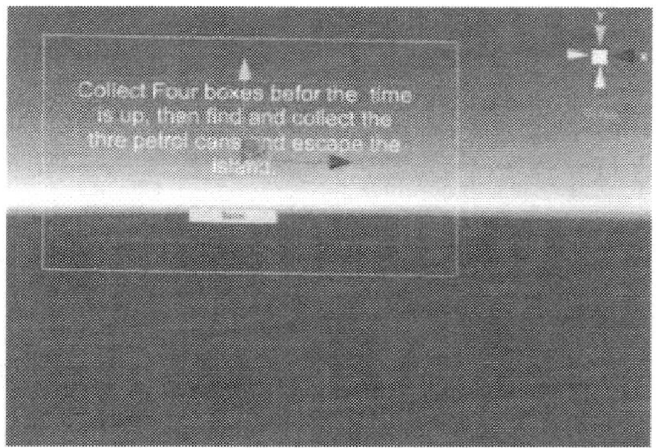

Figure 5-13: Moving the text above the button

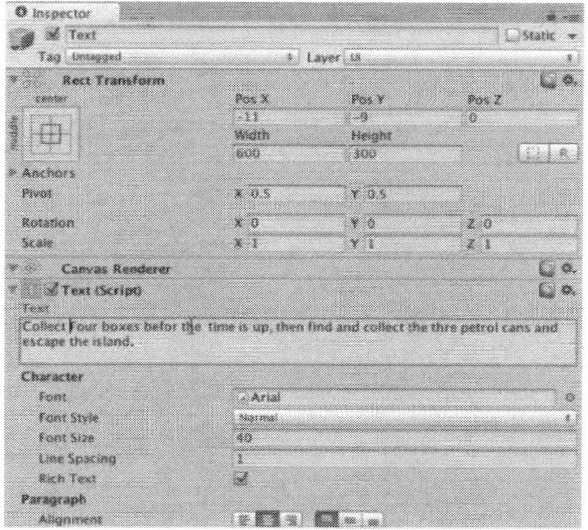

Figure 5-14: Setting-up the new text

- We can also change the label of the button, by modifying the text attribute of the **Text** object located within the **Button** object in the **Hierarchy** window.

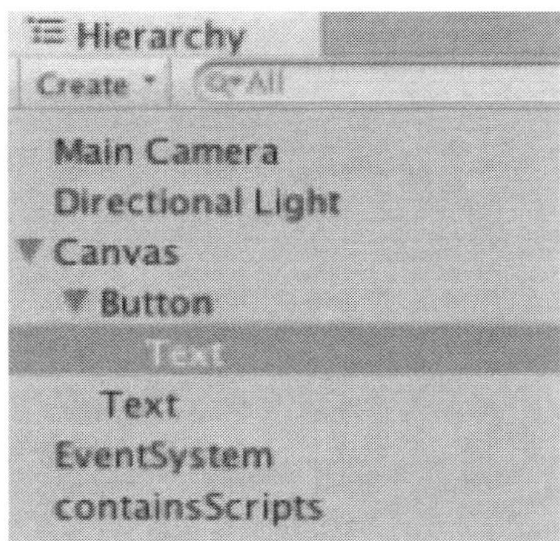

Figure 5-15: Selecting the text for the button

Once this object is selected, we can change its **text** attribute to >> **Click to Start** <<.

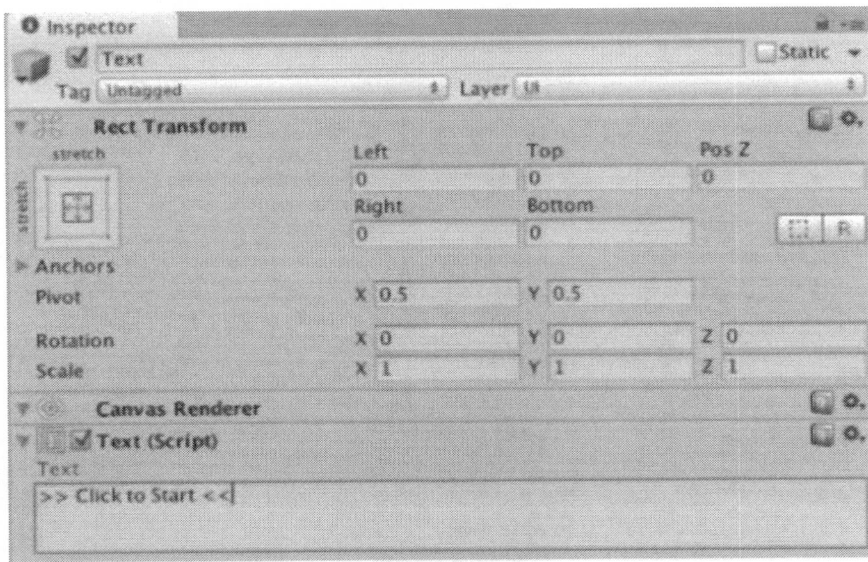

Figure 5-16: Modifying the Start button

- Save your scene and play it to see how the full game works.

DISPLAYING THE SCORE IN EACH SCENE

At present, while our game works properly, it would be great to display the score onscreen. So, first, let's display the score onscreen using the same technique that we have used before, that is: creating a **UI | Text** element, and changing its content from the script.

- Open the **indoor** scene.
- Create a new **UI | Text** object (**Game Object | UI | Text**).
- Rename this element **scoreUI**.
- Move it so that it appears in the top-right corner of the screen.
- Using the **Inspector** window, change its size or color as you wish (for example white).

At this stage, we just need to access this element from the script that counts the score, and to update its text accordingly every time the score is increased.

- Open the script **collectObjects_b** (i.e., the script linked to the **FPSController** that manages collisions).
- In this script, create a new function that will update the score as follows.

```
void updateScore ()
{
	GameObject.Find("scoreUI").GetComponent<Text>().text = "Score: "+score;
}
```

- In the function above, we access the game object **scoreUI**, and then modify its **text** attribute with the **score** that has just been changed (i.e., the value of the score is added to the text "**Score:**" to create a new value of type **String**).

Then, we will make sure that the UI for the score displays **0** initially.

- In the **Start** function, add the following code before the closing curly bracket for this function.

```
GameObject.Find("scoreUI").GetComponent<Text>().text = "";
```

- Add the following code within the **OnControllerColliderHit** function inside the conditional statement for the label **pick_me** (the new code is highlighted in bold).

```
print ("collision with "+ label);
score = score + 1;
updateScore();
```

- In the previous code, we just call the function **updateScore**, so that the score displayed onscreen is updated.
- Save your script.
- Switch to Unity, play the **indoor** scene, and check that the score is updated whenever the player picks-up a box.
- You can also open the **outdoor** scene, create a new text UI, rename it **scoreUI**, then test the scene, and check that the score is displayed and updated whenever the player picks-up a petrol can.

Displaying items collected as part of the user interface (using images)

At this stage, we have managed to display the score onscreen. However, it would also be great to display the number of petrol cans collected in the outdoor scene, instead of just using text. For this purpose, we will do the following:

- Import images.
- Add these images to the Graphical User Interface (GUI).
- Display an additional image for each petrol can that has been collected.

First, let's import the image that we will be using to represent the cans:

- Locate the resource pack that you have downloaded at the start of the book.
- In this resource pack, locate the image called **petrol_can** that is within the folder **images_and_textures**.
- Import this image in Unity: you can either use the option **Assets | Import**, or just drag and drop this file from the resource pack to one of the folders located in Unity's **Project** window.
- Once this is done, it is time to create a UI element.
- Open the **outdoor** scene (after saving the current scene, if necessary), if it is not already open.
- In this scene (i.e., the **outdoor** scene), create a new **Raw Image** element (**Game Object | UI | Raw Image**). This will create a **Raw Image** game object that is within a corresponding **Canvas** in the **Hierarchy** window.
- In the **Hierarchy** window, change the name of this game object from **Raw Image** to **item1**.

We now need to apply the image that we have imported (**petrol_can**) to this **Raw Image** object (i.e., **item1**):

- Select the game object **item1** in the **Hierarchy** window.
- Drag and drop the image **petrol_can** from the project window to the field called **Texture**, in the **RawImage** component for the game object **item1**, as highlighted on the next screenshot.

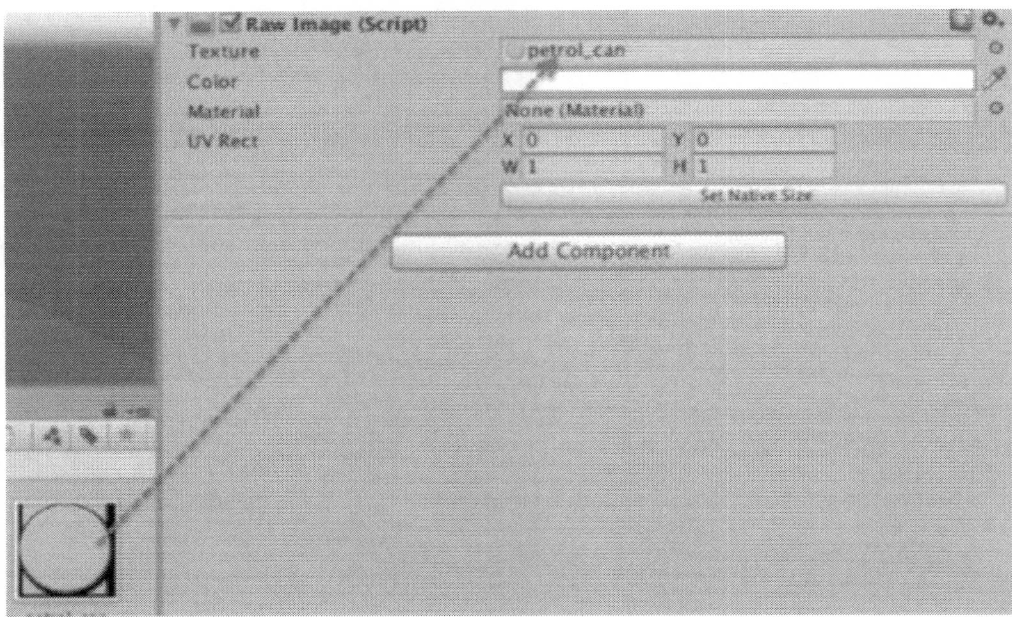

Figure 5-17: Adding an image to the GUI

- Switch to the **Scene** view.
- By default, the **item1** will be in the middle of the screen.

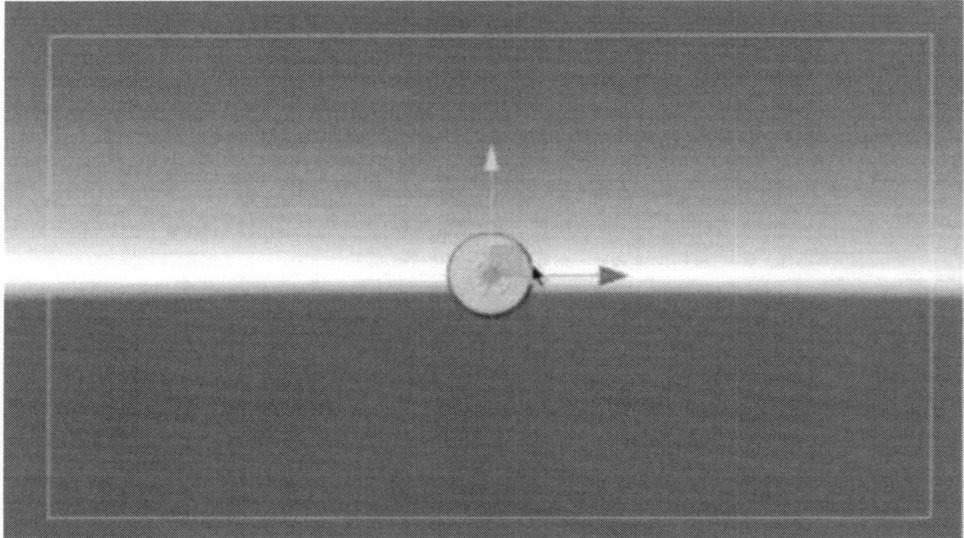

Figure 5-18: Adding the first image onscreen

- We will move this object to the bottom-left corner by either using the **Move** tool (the **W** key) and dragging both the red and green arms for this object, or (even better) by dragging the blue rectangle that corresponds to the plan defined by the x- and y-axes, as illustrated in the previous figure.
- Once this is done, you can switch to the **Game view**, to ensure that the image appears in the bottom-left corner of the screen.

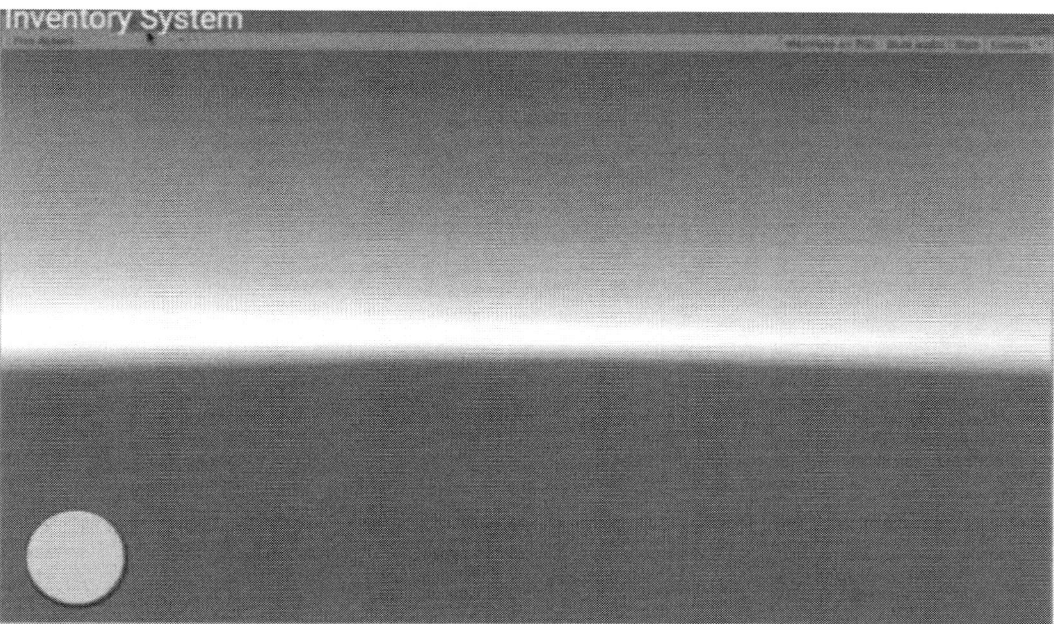

Figure 5-19: Displaying a simple inventory system

Next, we will duplicate this image three times, and place the duplicates to the right of the first image:

- Select the object **item1** in the **Hierarchy** window.
- Duplicate it three times using *CTRL + D*; as you do so, new objects will be created; please rename them**item2**, **item3**, and **item4** (i.e., Unity will append a number to each of the duplicates automatically).
- Using the **Move** tool, move the duplicates along the x-axis so that the distance between each of them is constant, as illustrated on the next figure.

Figure 5-20: Adding three icons

Now that we have defined these four images, and placed them on the user interface, it is time to control when and how they will be displayed using a script.

- Open the script **collectObjects_b**.
- Add the following code at the beginning of the class.

```
GameObject item1;
GameObject item2;
GameObject item3;
GameObject item4;
```

- In the previous lines of code, we declare four public game objects; these are public variables; this means that we will be able to access them through the **Inspector** window (e.g., drag and drop objects to these variables in the **Inspector** window).
- Please add the following code in the **Start** function.

```
if (SceneManager.GetActiveScene().name == "outdoor")
{
        item1 = GameObject.Find("item1");
        item2 = GameObject.Find("item2");
        item3 = GameObject.Find("item3");
        item4 = GameObject.Find("item4");

        item1.SetActive(false);
        item2.SetActive(false);
        item3.SetActive(false);
        item4.SetActive(false);
}
```

- This code is executed only if we are currently in the **outdoor** scene; this is because this script is also used in the **indoor** scene; however, the **indoor** scene does not include any of these items (i.e., **item1**, **item2**, etc.). This being said, you could, if you wished, create the items item1-2-3-4 in the **indoor** scene too.
- In the previous code, we do generally two things for each object: we link the variable (e.g., **item1**) to the object they correspond to and we deactivate the corresponding object then. This will deactivate the four images that we have initially set-up on the GUI (i.e., **item1**, **item2**, **item3**, and **item4**). They will, therefore, be invisible, unless we activate them.
- The last thing we need to do now is to activate each of these images as we collect petrol cans. So, for example, as the number of petrol cans collected increases, we will activate (i.e., display) **item1**, then **item2**, and so on.

Let's add the last part of the script.

- In the function **OnControllerColliderHit**, and within the conditional statement starting with **if (label == petrol_can)**, add the following code (changes are highlighted in bold).

```
if (label == "petrol_can")
{
        nbPetrolCansCollected = nbPetrolCansCollected + 1;
        if (nbPetrolCansCollected == 1) item1.SetActive(true);
        if (nbPetrolCansCollected == 2) item2.SetActive(true);
        if (nbPetrolCansCollected == 3) item3.SetActive(true);
        if (nbPetrolCansCollected == 4) item4.SetActive(true);
        updateScore();
```

In the previous code:

- If the variable **nbPetrolCansCollected** equals to 1 then we activate **item1**.
- If the variable **nbPetrolCansCollected** equals to 2 then we activate **item2**.
- The same applies to the two other images and objects.

That's it. So, you can now save your script and check that this new feature works for the **outdoor** scene.

You can, of course, replace the image used to represent the number of cans collected (i.e., **petrol_can**) with any image of your choice, and resize it accordingly.

ADDING SOUND EFFECTS

In this section, we will just add sound effects whenever the player picks-up an object. Providing feedback to users is always a good idea, and this feedback can be provided in many forms, including using audio.

For this we will be using **Audio Source** and **Audio Clip** components. An **Audio Source** is a bit like a sound system (or MP3 player) with a charger for different CDs or songs. By default, the **FPSController** includes an **Audio Source** and plays a clip for each footstep. However, for this section, we would like to temporarily change the sound played by the **Audio Source**, to play, instead, a sound effect whenever an object has been picked-up.

For this, we will do the following:

- Import a sound effect.
- Select this sound effect as the "tune" to be played on the sound system (i.e., **Audio Clip**).
- Play the sound effect whenever the player picks-up an object.

So let's get started!

- Open the script **collectObjects_b**;
- Add the following code to the beginning of the script.

```
public AudioClip pickupSound;
```

- This code creates a placeholder for the **Audio Clip** that we want to play.
- Modify the code in the function **OnControllerColliderHit**, as highlighted in the next code snippet.

```
Destroy (hit.collider.gameObject);
gameObject.GetComponent<AudioSource>().clip= pickupSound;
gameObject.GetComponent<AudioSource>().Play();
```

In the previous code, we access the **Audio Source** component of the object linked to this script (i.e., the **FPSController**), we set the clip to be played (i.e., **pickupSound**), and we then play it.

Please save your script (*CTRL + S*). Once this is done, we just need to set the variable **pickupSound** to the **Audio Clip** that we have imported previously.

- Locate where you have downloaded your resource pack.
- Locate the file **pick_up.wav**, in the folder labeled **sounds**, within the resource pack.

- Import this sound to your Unity project by dragging and dropping this file to Unity's **Project** folder.
- Select the object **FPSController** in the **Hierarchy**.
- In the **Inspector**, look at the script component **collectObjects_b**, and you should notice an empty field called **pickupSound**.
- Drag and drop the clip you have imported (i.e., **pick_up**) to this **placeholder**, as illustrated on the next figure.

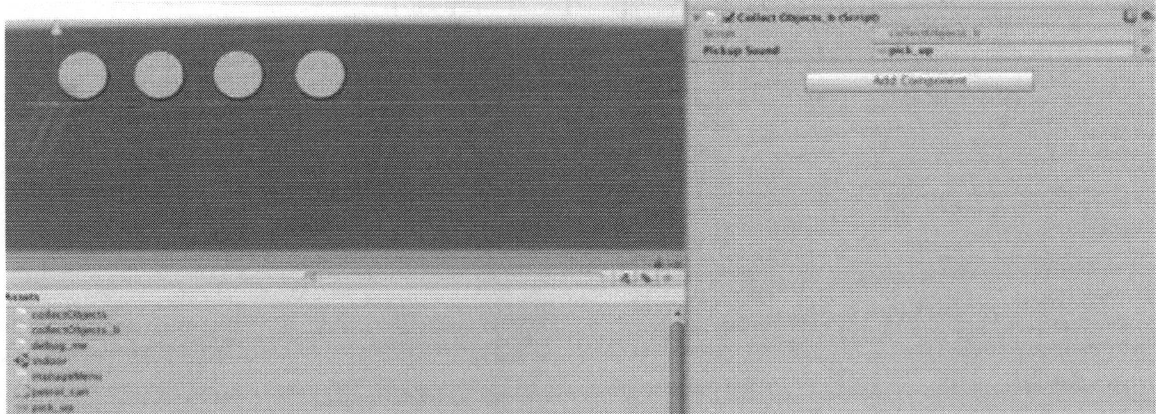

Figure 5-21: Adding a new Audio Clip

Now that this has been done, we just need to perform the same for the outdoor scene. Please save the current scene (i.e., **indoor**), open the **outdoor** scene and repeat the steps that you have just performed (e.g., drag and drop the clip you have imported to this **placeholder)**.

That's about it!

- Save your code.
- Switch to Unity.
- Play both scenes (outdoor or indoor) and check that the sound is played accordingly whenever you collect items.

> Although you have been using a sound available in the resource pack, you can also create your own sound for your game. The site http://www.bfxr.net makes it possible to create your own sounds easily by just using click.

PLAYING A BACKGROUND MUSIC

At this stage, you are probably very comfortable with adding sounds, and we will perform this task again, but this time, for a background sound. The process will be to:

- Create an empty object.
- Rename this object **manageAudio**.
- Add an **Audio Source** component to this object (**Component | Audio | Audio Source**).
- Add a script to this object that controls whether the player can mute this background sound.

So let's get started!

- Open the **indoor** scene.
- Create an empty object (**Game Object | Create Empty**).
- Rename this object **manageAudio**.
- Add an **Audio Source** component to this object (**Component | Audio | Audio Source**).

Next, we can add a new clip as part of the **Audio Source**, so that we can play it:

- Locate the folder that you have downloaded for the resource pack.
- Locate the file **indoor_bg_sound.wav** (within the folder sounds). All background sounds included in the folder **sounds** (except for pick-up.wav) have been created by Kevin McLeod and are royalty-free. You can also download and use more sounds from his **official website**.
- Import this file in Unity.
- Drag and drop this file in the **AudioClip** attribute of the **Audio Source** component for the object **manageAudio**.
- For the **Audio Source** component, keep the option **Play On Awake** checked, so that the sound (i.e., clip) is played immediately when the scene has been loaded.
- So that this sound is played in a loop, we can also check the box labeled **Loop** for the corresponding **Audio Source** component.
- You can also, if you wish, modify the volume of the sound.
- Play the scene and check that the background sound is played.

At this stage, we have managed to play the background sound; however, it would be great to make it possible for the player to mute this sound. This is a common feature in games and a good design practice to give more choice to players. So, what we could do next is to allocate a key (for example **P**) to the sound, so that whenever the player presses this key, the sound is toggled to the states **ON** or **OFF**. To do so, we need to do the following:

- Detect that the key **P** has been pressed.
- Create a variable that will determine whether the sound should be **ON** or **OFF**.
- Start or stop the sound based on the variable defined above.

So let's get started:

- In the **Project** window, create a new script (**Create | C# Script**).
- Rename this script **toggleAudio**.
- Open this script and include the following code.

```
bool soundOn;
void Start ()
{
	soundOn=true;
}

void Update ()
{
	if (Input.GetKeyDown(KeyCode.P))
	{
		soundOn = !soundOn;
		if (soundOn) gameObject.GetComponent<AudioSource>().Play();
		else gameObject.GetComponent<AudioSource>().Stop();
	}
}
```

In the previous code, we detect whether the key P is pressed. If this is the case, then we change the value of the variable **soundOn**: it is set to true it was previously false, and it is set to false if it was previously true.

The operator **!** is a **logical not** operator, which means, in simple terms, the opposite value. Since a Boolean variable can only have two values: if it is not true then it is false, and if is not false, then it is true.

After changing the value of the variable **soundOn**, we can either play or stop the sound.

- Save your code.

- Add the script **toggleAudio** to the object **manageAudio** (i.e., drag and drop the script on the object).
- Play the scene.
- Press the **P** key several times, and check that the background sound is either muted or played.

At this stage, we have managed to play the background sound and we were also able to mute it, if necessary. So, we could possibly do the same for the **outdoor** scene. A simple way to do this would be to create an empty object in the **outdoor** scene and repeat the steps performed in the last section. However, we could make our code more efficient.

How you may ask?

Well, instead of recreating similar objects and code, we could just try to keep the object **manageAudio** across scenes, so that it is kept whenever we load the outdoor scene.

By default, Unity will not keep any of the objects created in the indoor scene as we load the next scene. So we need to tell Unity to keep this particular object and not to destroy it whenever we load a new scene. Thankfully, there is a function that does just that, and it is called **DontDestroyOnLoad**. This function, when added to a script that is linked to an object, makes sure that this object is not destroyed when a new scene is loaded.

So in our case, we need to use this function in the script **toggleAudio** (which is linked to the object **manageAudio)**.

So let's try this:

- Open the script **toggleAudio**.
- Add the following code to it (at the end of the script).

```
void Awake()
{
	DontDestroyOnLoad (transform.gameObject);
}
```

In the previous code, we use the function **Awake**, which is called before the game starts. In this function, we specify that the game object linked to this script should not be destroyed when a new scene is loaded.

- Save your code.
- Switch to Unity.
- Check the build settings (i.e., that both **indoor** and **outdoor** scenes are included in the build settings, using the menu **File | Build Settings**).

- Open the **indoor** scene.
- Play the **indoor** scene.
- Collect four or more boxes.
- As the **outdoor** scene is loaded, try to mute or play the background sound using the **P** key.

ADDING A MINI-MAP

Now that we have added a background sound, it would be great for our player to know where he or she is in relation to the environment, and a mini-map, in this case, would be useful. By mini-map we mean an outline of the scene displayed on top of the game. Mini-maps are usually a simplified representation of the environment, and display the position of the player (usually symbolized by a dot), the position of the NPCs (also symbolized by dots), along with the position of important items such as ammunitions or health packs.

So how do we create a mini-map?

Well, it should be relatively simple, as we have, so far, looked at all the elements that we need to create this map. The process will be as follows:

- Create a camera.
- Display the image captured by this camera in the top-right corner of the screen.
- Identify the objects that we would like to be displayed on the mini-map.
- Create corresponding icons (e.g., red or green dots).
- Allocate these icons to a specific layer (we will explore this concept in the next paragraphs).
- Make sure that the camera allocated for the mini-map only displays items that have been linked to that layer: in other words we are selective as to what we would like to capture (and display) with this camera.

So let's get started:

- Open the **outdoor** scene.
- Create a new camera (**GameObject | Camera**).
- Rename this camera **top_view**.
- Drag and drop this camera on the object **FPSController**, so that the camera becomes a child of this object (i.e., this camera will move along with the player).

Select this camera and perform the next modifications using the **Inspector** window.

- Set the **Position** of the camera **top_view** to **(0, 20, 0)** so that it is just above the player.
- Set the **Rotation** attributes to **(90, 0, 0)** so that it faces downwards.

- For this camera (**top_view**), in the **ViewPort Rect** section of the **Camera** component, set the **x** attribute to **.75** and the **y** attribute to **.75**.
- In the **ViewPort Rect** section of the **Camera** component, set the **width** to **.25**, and the **Height** to .25.
- Set the **Depth** of the camera to **1** so that the image it captures is displayed on top of the game (i.e., atop the image captured by the other camera embedded on the **FPScontroller**).
- Test the game to ensure that you can see the mini-map, as illustrated in the next figure.

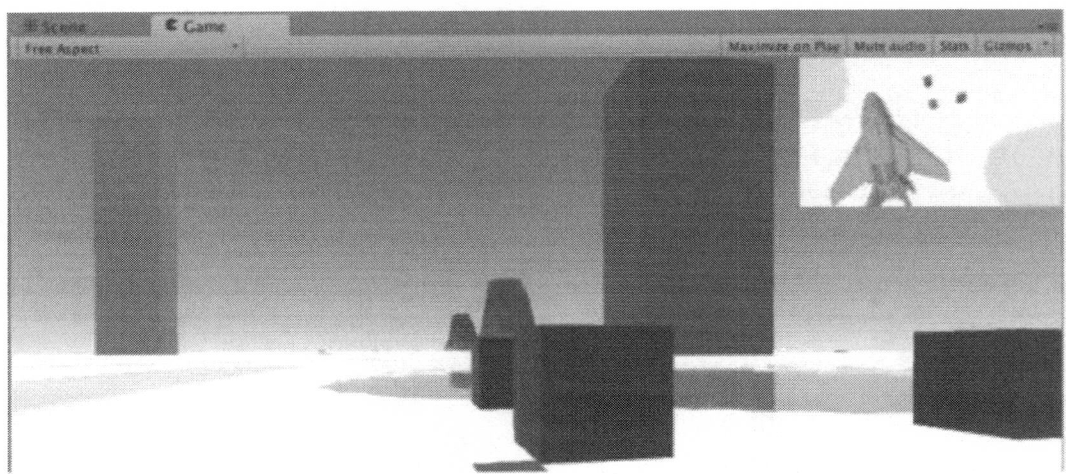

Figure 5-22: Displaying a simple mini-map

At this stage we have a mini-map, located in the top-right corner of the screen, that displays the environment around the player. As it is, it works perfectly; however, it would be great to also locate elements on this map with red or green dots, such as the plane or the petrol cans. So, we will add these to the map, and the process will be as follows:

- Create dots that will be placed above each of the important objects.
- Add these dots to a particular layer.
- Make sure that the **top_view** camera (used for the mini-map) only displays objects that are on this layer (e.g., dots), in addition to the terrain.
- Make sure that the main camera (the one attached to the **First-Person Controller**) does not display these dots.

First, let's create these dots:

- Create a new sphere (**Game Object | 3D Object | Sphere**).

- Check that its **scale** attribute is set to **(1, 1, 1)**.
- Create a new **green** material and apply it to this sphere (i.e., select **Create | Material** from the **Project** window and drag and drop this new material to the object).
- Rename the sphere **green_dot**.
- Drag and drop this sphere on top of the object **FPSController**, so that the sphere becomes a child of the **FPSController**.
- When this is done, select the object **green_dot**, and change its position to **(0, 10, 0)**. This means that it will be 10 meters above the player.
- Select this object (i.e., **green_dot**).
- In the **Inspector**, click on the drop-down menu to the right of the label **Layer.**

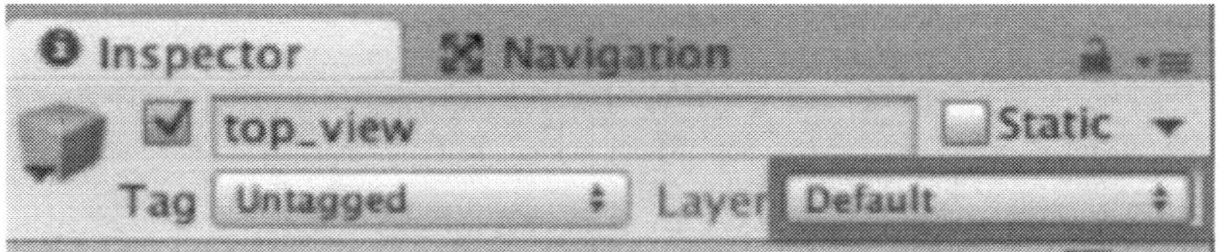

Figure 5-23: Adding and allocating a new layer for the dots

- Then select **Add Layer** from the drop-down menu.
- This will make it possible to create and allocate a layer for these dots.

In the new window, you will see a section of built-in layers, as well a custom layers named **User Layer 8**, **User Layer 9**, and so on. We will modify some of the user layers.

- Click to the right of the first user layer (for example **User Layer 8**), and type the text **mini-map** in the corresponding empty field.

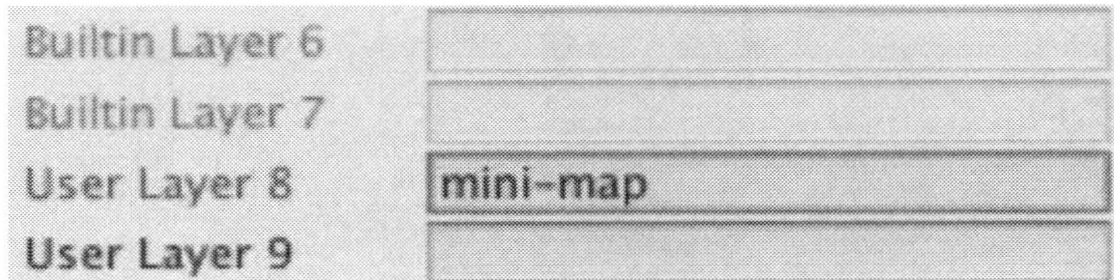

Figure 5-24: Adding a new layer

- Then press enter.

- Select the **green_dot** object in the **Hierarchy**; then, in the **Inspector** window, click on the drop-down menu to the right of the label **Layer**, and this time, you should see and select the layer that we have just created: **mini-map**.

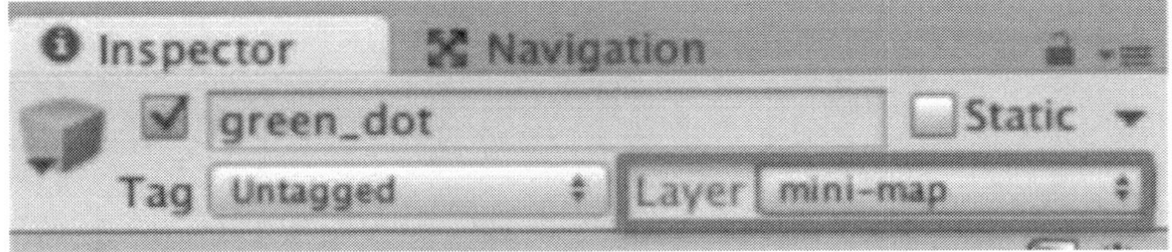

Figure 5-25: Adding a layer to the dot

At this stage, we have specified that the object **green_dot** is on the layer **mini-map**. We just need to make sure that it is not rendered by the main camera (i.e., the camera that is attached to the **FPSController** by default); so we will specify that the main camera should render all layers, except from the layer **mini-map** (as objects on the layer mini-map will be displayed by the **top_view** camera only).

- In the **Hierarchy** window, click on the object **FirstPersonCharacter**, that is within the object **FPS Controller**. It is important that you select the object **FirstPersonCharacter** because it includes a camera that we need to access.
- In the **Inspector** window, locate the **Camera** component for this object.
- In the **Culling Mask** section for this component, click on the drop-down menu to uncheck the option **mini-map**. This means that the camera will display all layers except from the layer **mini-map**.

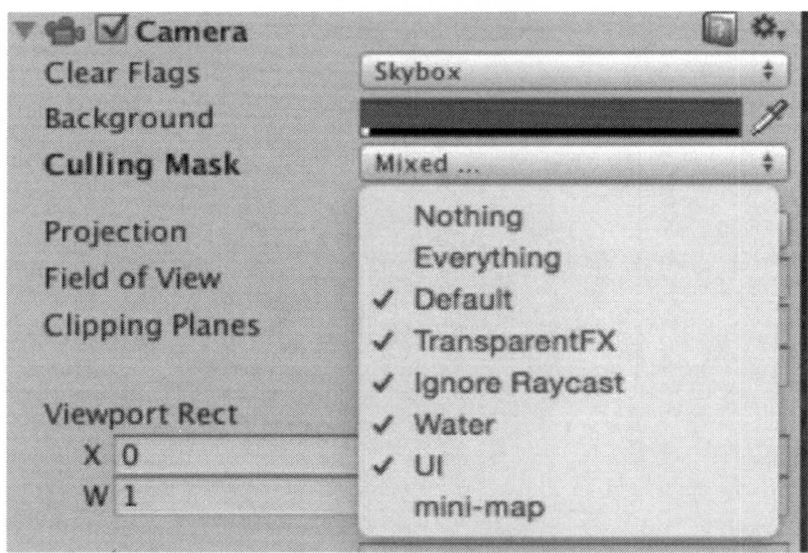

Figure 5-26: Rendering all layers except from the mini-map

We now need to specify that our mini-map (**top_view** camera) should display all objects on the layer **mini-map**; to do so, we will proceed as for the the previous steps:

- Select the camera **top_view** that is within the object **FPSController** in the **Hierarchy**.
- In the **Inspector** window, locate the component **Camera** for this object.
- Change the **Culling Mask** so that it only displays objects that are on the layer **mini-map**: for this you can choose the option **Nothing** first for the **Culling Mask**, this will clear the list of layers rendered by this camera, and then select the option **mini-map** from the same list, so that only the **mini-map** layer is selected. To display more detail you can choose to display more layers on this map, including the **Water** layer for example.

Now that you have managed to set-up the dot representing the First-Person Controller on the mini-map, please repeat the previous steps to add red and yellow dots, this time for petrol cans and the plane, respectively.

- Create a new sphere (**GameObject | 3D Object | Sphere**).
- Rename it **red_dot1**.
- Create a new **red** material (from the **Project** window, select: **Create | Material**)
- Apply this material to the sphere **red_dot1**.
- Duplicate this sphere twice. Rename these duplicates: **red_dot2** and **red_dot3**.
- Drag and drop each of the duplicates on each of the petrol cans.
- Once this is done, you should have one red dot for each petrol can.
- Change the position of each of these dots to **(0, 10, 0)**. To speed-up this process, you can search for the term **red_dot** in the **Hierarchy** search window, select all three objects matching this keyword (i.e., **red_dot1**, **red_dot2**, and **red_dot3**), and change their x, y, and z attributes simultaneously in the **Inspector** window to **(0, 10, 0)** and their layer to **mini-map**, as described on the next screenshot.

If you select several objects and then look at the **Inspector** window, you will see that attributes that are not the same for all these objects will be marked as -, while other attributes that are the same across all selected objects will be displayed. For example, on the next screenshot, we have selected the three red dots (i.e., **red_dot1**, **red_dot2**, and **red_dot3**) and we can look at the **Inspector** window to see their properties. The three objects selected have a different name (the name is not displayed in the **Inspector**); however, they all are selected (the check box is visible), they all are **Untagged** and on the layer **mini-map**. They also have the exact same position (relative to their respective parent). The object **red_dot1** is 10 meter above the first petrol can (which is its parent); the object **red_dot2** is 10 meter above the second petrol can (which is its parent), and the object **red_dot3** is 10 meter above the third petrol can (which is its parent).

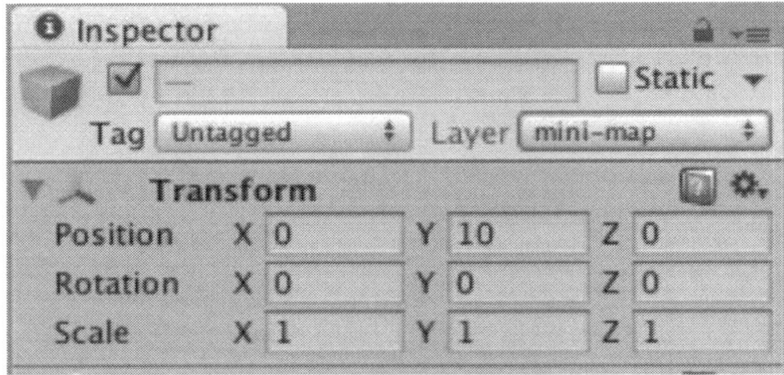

Figure 5-27: Modifying the position of the red dots

We can now create a yellow dot for the plane:

- Create a yellow dot (i.e., new sphere with a yellow color).
- Duplicate it, and rename each of these dots **yellow_dot1** and **yellow_dot2**.
- Drag the object **yellow_dot1** on the object called **plane**, drag the object **yellow_dot2** on the object called **AircraftJet**, and change the position of these objects (i.e., **yellow_dot1** and **yellow_dot2**) to **(0, 10, 0)** and their layer to **mini-map**.
- Play the scene and test that all these items appear on the mini-map and not on the main camera, as described on the next figure.
- Et voila!

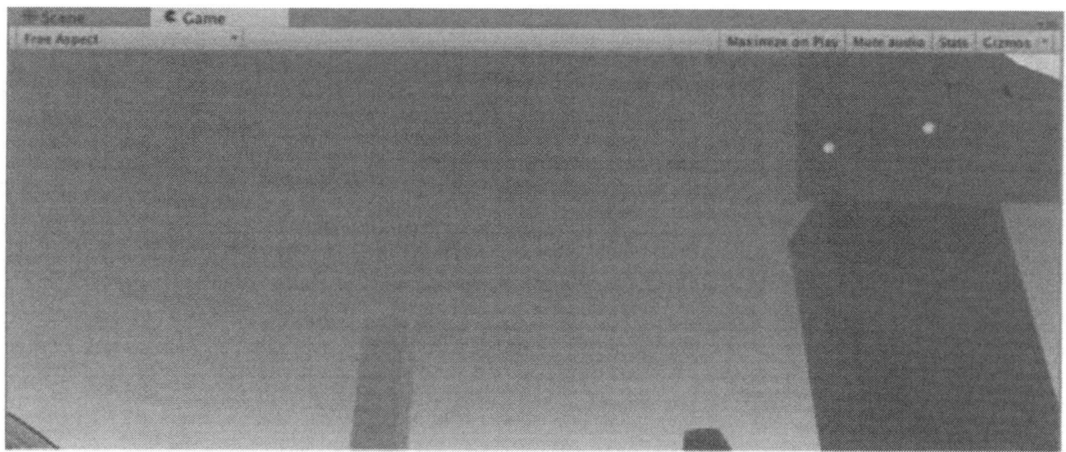

Figure 5-28: Displaying a mini-map with dots

Now, there is a last cool thing we could do; that is, to be able to toggle the map when the player presses the key *M*. So the idea is to hide or display the map accordingly; for this, we will go through the following steps:

- Detect when the key *M* is pressed.
- Change the value of a Boolean variable called **displayMiniMap**.
- Disable or enable the camera based on the value of this variable (i.e., true or false).

So, let's try this:

- Open the **outdoor** scene.
- Create a new script.
- Rename this script **toggleCamera**.
- Drag and drop this script from the **Project** window to the object called **top_view** (i.e., camera) that is within the object **FPSController**, in the **Hierarchy**.

Once this done, modify the script as follows:

```
Camera topCamera;
bool displayCamera;
void Start ()
{
        topCamera = GetComponent<Camera>();
        displayCamera = true;
}

void Update ()
{
        if (Input.GetKeyDown(KeyCode.M))
        {
                displayCamera = !displayCamera;
                if (displayCamera) topCamera.enabled = true;
                else topCamera.enabled = false;
        }
}
```

In the previous code:

- We first declare a variable **topCamera** that will be referring to the camera used for the top view.
- When the *M* key is pressed, we will enable or disable the camera, based on the value of the variable **displayCamera**.
- Please save your script.
- Play the scene and check that pressing the *M* key successively deactivates and activates the top-view camera (i.e., the mini-map).

LEVEL ROUNDUP

In this chapter, we have learned how to polish-up our game by adding sound, displaying a simple inventory system, a mini-map, the score, and a splash-screen. We became more comfortable with functions, variables, and components' properties. We managed to detect users' key input and to interact accordingly (i.e., by muting the sound or hiding the map). So, again, we have covered considerable ground to produce a relatively polished game with some of the key features that you will find in many 3D games.

Checklist

You can consider moving to the next stage if you can do the following:

- Detect keystrokes form the script.
- Play and stop a sound from the script.
- Load scenes.
- Keep objects from being destroyed after loading a new scene.
- Display text onscreen using UI elements.
- Attach a script to an object.
- Update UI elements.
- Tell the difference between an **Audio Source** and an **Audio Clip**.
- Activate and deactivate a camera from a script.

Quiz

Now, let's check your knowledge! Please answer the following questions by specifying whether the statements are TRUE or FALSE. The answers are on the next page.

1. The function **DontDestroyOnLoad** is used so that objects are not destroyed when the player collides with them.
2. The following code will detect if the key *E* is pressed.

```
void Update()
{
        if (Input.GetKeyDown (E))
        {
                print ("The Key E was pressed");
        }
}
```

3. Find and write the missing code below so that the script makes it possible to empty the text from a **Text UI** game object called **uiText**.

```
void Start()
{
        GameObject t;
        <MISSING CODE>
}
```

4. By default, the option **Play on Awake** is set to true for all **Audio Source** components.
5. Typing the keyword **scenes** in the search field within the **Project** window will list and display all scenes in the current project.
6. A camera can only display one layer onscreen.
7. If the scene **scene5** has been added to the build settings, the following code will load it.

```
SceneManager.LoadTheScene("scene5");
```

8. What could this error message mean, based on the code below **"The best method overload for function ... is not compatible"**.

   a) The parameter passed to the function does not match the type that is required.
   b) Your computer is not compatible with MonoDevelop.
   c) There is a system overload due to lack of memory and the code in the function can't be processed.

9. What does this error message mean based on the code below **"Expecting } found..."**.

   a) The code for your function needs to be ended by a closing curly bracket.

b) The code for your conditional statement starts with an opening curly bracket and needs to be ended by a closing curly bracket.
c) All of the above.

10. What three shortcuts can you use to consecutively save your code, switch to Unity, and then play the scene?

a) *CTRL +S, ALT + Tab, CTRL + P.*
b) *CTRL +S, CTRL + D, CTRL + P.*
c) *CTRL +S, CTRL + D, CTRL + R*

Solutions to the Quiz

1. FALSE
2. FALSE; it should be as follows

```
        if (Input.GetKeyDown (KeyCode.E))
        {
                print ("The Key E was pressed");
        }
}
```

3.

```
void Start()
{
        GameObject t;
        t.GetComponent<Text>().text = "";
}
```

4. TRUE.
5. FALSE (**t:scene** is correct)
6. FALSE
7. FALSE
8. a
9. c
10. a

Challenge 1

Now that you have managed to complete this chapter and that you have improved your skills, you could use these to improve the flow of your game. So for this challenge, you will be creating an instruction screen and a game-over screen.

- Create two additional scenes: a briefing and debriefing screen for the first scene.
- Link these scenes, so that the player first reads the instructions, then after clicking a button, moves to the briefing screen, then to the first level (indoor scene). After completing the indoor scene, a debriefing screen should be displayed, congratulating the player and also explaining what should be done in the outdoor level.
- All screens can be created with UI components (e.g., text, buttons, or raw images).
- **Only if you have time**: Whenever the player has managed to fly the plane, a **win** screen is loaded after 4 seconds.

Challenge 2

Here, you will modify your game so that if the player runs out of time, s/he should be taken to the game-over screen.

- Create a **game-over** scene.
- In the first level, if the time is over, the **game-over** scene should be loaded.

6

Adding and Managing Simple Artificial Intelligence

In this section we will discover how to add NPCs and give them basic intelligence so that they can follow the player and also follow a particular path that we would have defined.

After completing this chapter, you will be able to:

- Add and control a Non-Player Character (NPC).
- Control NPCs so that they look for and follow the player.
- Create a simple path and get the NPCs to follow this path.
- Detect collision between the NPCs and the player.
- Understand and use Navmesh navigation.
- Understand and apply basic Artificial Intelligence (AI) to NPCs.

ADDING AND SETTING-UP OUR FIRST NPC

As it is, the game is quite interesting; however it would be great to add a bit of challenge for the player, in addition to exploring the scenes and finding objects.

So, what about adding Non-Player Characters (NPCs)?!

In this section, we will get to add NPCs using Unity's built-in assets, and configure them so that they look for and follow the player.

First, let's add an NPC to the scene.

- Open the **indoor** scene.
- You may deactivate the **ceiling** object so that it is easier to add objects to the scene.
- You can set the **Ambient Light Intensity** to **1**, so that it is easier to see the scene (**Window | Lighting | Settings**).
- You can also display the view from above by clicking on the green arm (y-axis) of the gizmo.
- Open the **Project** window, and navigate to the folder: **Standard Assets | Characters | ThirdPersonCharacter| Prefabs**.
- In this folder, you should see two objects; one of them should be labeled **AIThirdPersonController**. It corresponds to a character that you can use as an NPC (after some light configuration).
- Drag and drop this prefab (i.e., **AIThirdPersonController**) to the scene, and place it just above the ground, relatively away from the player, so that it needs to cover some distance to get near the player.
- This should create a new object in the **Hierarchy** window called **AIThirdPersonController**.
- Once this is done, click once on this object in the **Hierarchy** and then look at the **Inspector** window.
- This should display all components for this object, and you should see, amongst other things, that it includes a component called **AICharacterControl**, as illustrated on the next figure.

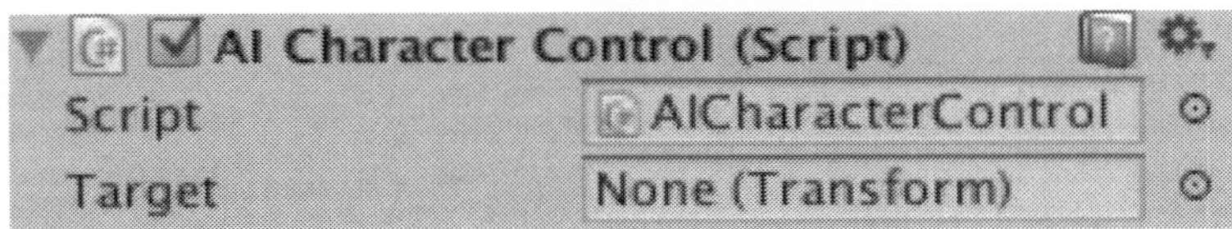

Figure 6-1: Controlling the AI with a script

- As you can see, this component is a script with a public variable called **Target**. This variable **Target** is empty for now, and its type is **Transform**. The **Target** variable is linked to the target for the NPC. So, by specifying the target we can effectively tell Unity what object the NPC will be following (or targeting). The only thing we need to do is to drag and drop the object that we want the NPC to follow on top of this field (i.e., **Target**). In our case, the target is the player. So we need to drag and drop the object for the player (the object labeled **FPSController;** this object is located in the **maze** folder within the **Hierarchy** window), to this empty field.
- So, let's proceed: Select the object **AIThirdPersonController.**
- Drag and drop the object **FPSController** from the **Hierarchy** window to the empty field to the right of the variable **Target,** located in the **AICharacterControl** component of the object **AIThirdPersonController**.

Once this is done, the **Target** field for the object **AICharacterControl** should look as follows:

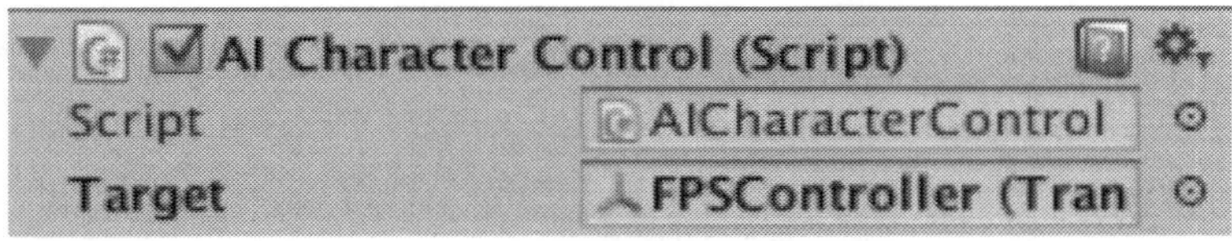

Figure 6-2: Specifying a target for the NPC

Now, if we play the scene as it is, you should see that the NPC still does not move, although we have set a target. The reason for this is that, at this stage, the NPC does not "know" how to get to the player. So, some computations need to be performed so that Unity determines possible routes and nodes that the NPC can use to get (i.e., navigate) to its target. This is performed using the **Navigation** window. So let's have a look at this window and finalize the navigation for the NPC.

- Open the **Navigation** window (**Window | Navigation**).
- This should open the window **Navigation** next to the **Inspector** window.

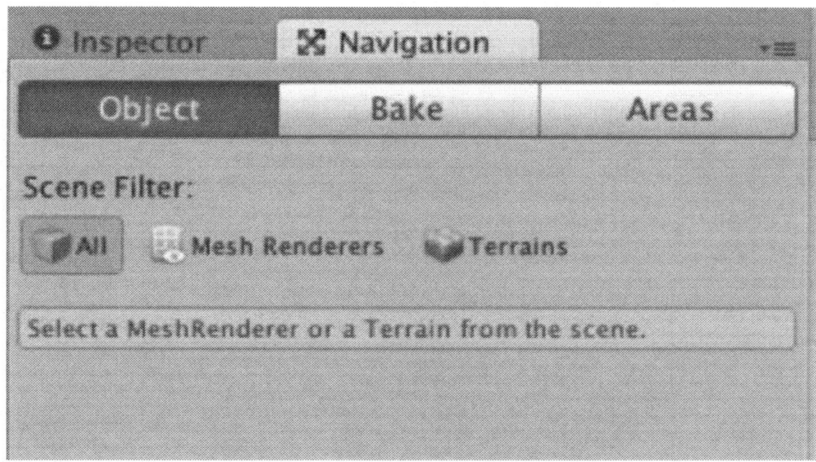

Figure 6-3: The Navigation window

The idea now is to specify all objects that the NPC will be able to walk on or avoid, in order to get to the player. To do so, we will need to select these (e.g., in the **Hierarchy** window), specify that the NPC can either walk on or around these objects, and then "Bake" the scene. The "Baking" process will calculate possible "routes" that the NPC can take in order to reach its target. So, let's try this:

- Select the ground object in the **Hierarchy** window.
- In the **Navigation** window, select the option **Static Mesh**, and leave the option **Navigation Area** to **Walkable** (i.e., default option).

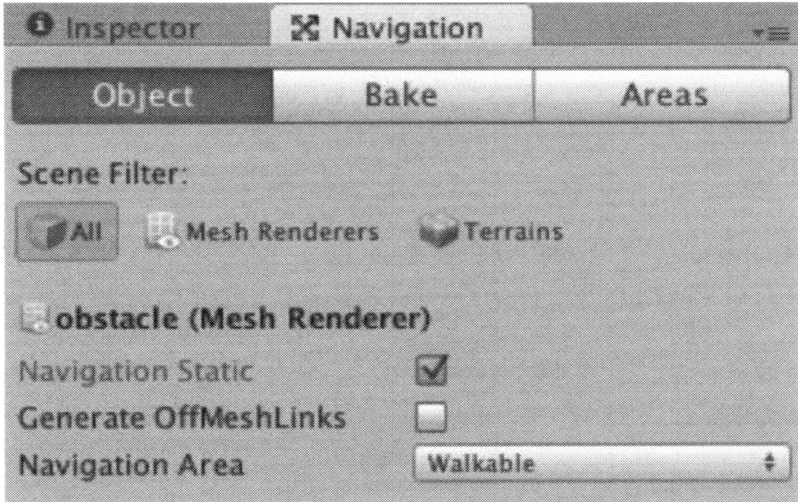

Figure 6-4: "Baking" the scene – part1

- Once this is done, click on the button labeled **Bake** located at the bottom of the **Navigation** window.

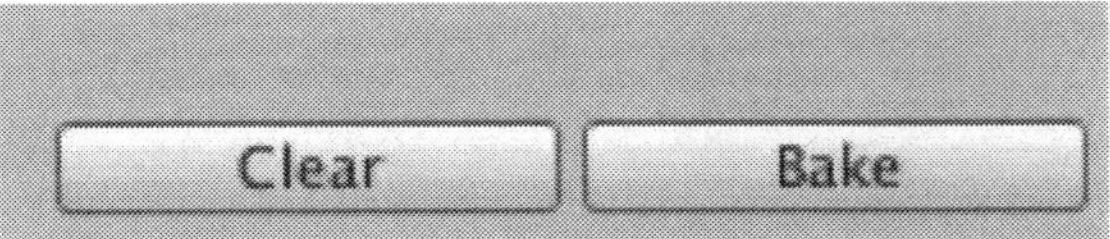

Figure 6-5: Baking the scene - part2

- This should display a progress bar, at the bottom of the **Navigation** window, that will disappear once the baking process is complete. At this stage, if you look at the ground, you should see that it looks blue, and that Unity has generated a few nodes (i.e., black dots).

We are almost there, as we just need to repeat the last steps with the other objects present in the scene, including walls and objects to collect (but not the player). Please do the following:

- Select each wall in the scene, as well as the collectable objects. To speed-up the process, you can also, in the **Hierarchy** window, search for the term **cube**, and this will return all cubes included in the scene (i.e., including walls and collectable objects). You can then select all these objects (e.g., using *CTRL + Click*).
- Then select the option **Navigation Static** in the **Navigation** window.
- Leave the other options as default and click on the button labeled **Bake**.

The **Scene** view may now look as follows:

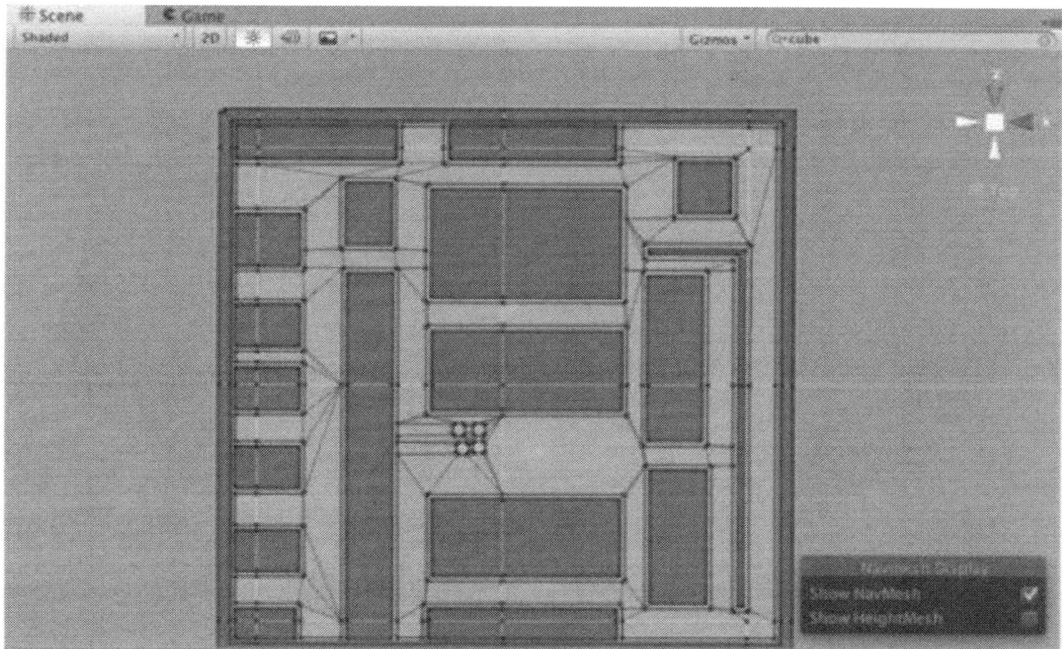

Figure 6-6: Displaying meshes and nodes after "Baking" the scene

At this stage we are ready to test our game:

- Please play the scene.
- Look at the **Scene** view.
- See how the NPC is finding its way to the player.

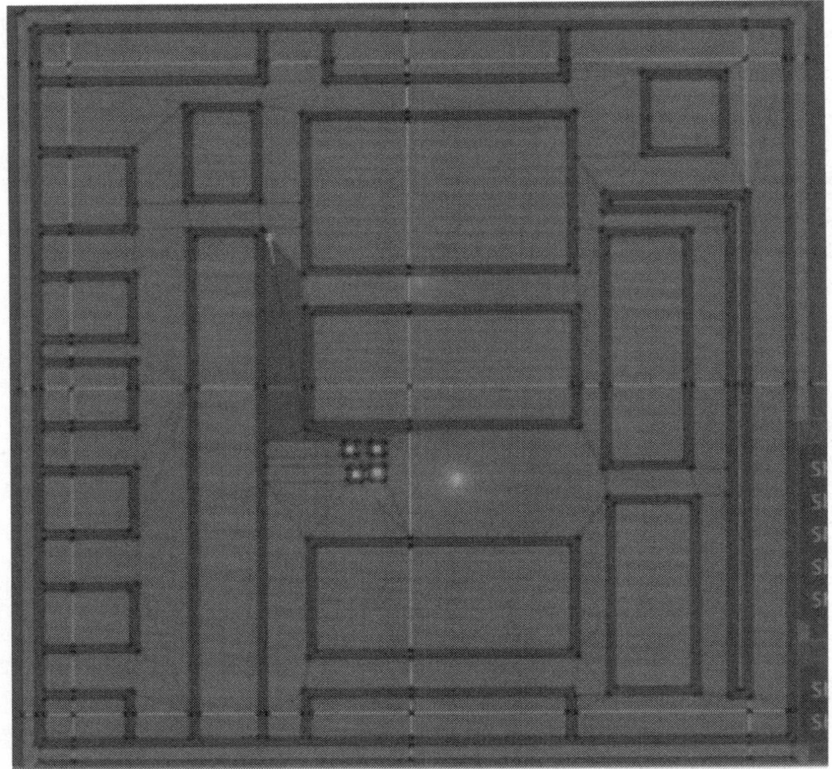

Figure 6-7: The NPC navigating towards the player

CREATING A PATH FOR OUR NPC

Ok, so at this stage, our NPC can look for and find the player; however, it would also be great to be able to have an NPC that walks on a predefined path. This path could, for example, be defined by three or four points that the NPC will try to reach successively. For example, it could go from point1, to point2, to point3, and then to point4. In terms of game programming, these points are often called **waypoints**, or **reference points**. So, in our case the process will be as follows:

- Create four new waypoints (or reference points).
- Give a rank or index to these points (e.g., **target1**, **target2**, **target3**, and **target4**).
- Then get the NPC to look for and reach each of these targets sequentially.
- Whenever the NPC is close to the waypoint it is targeting, it will start to look for the next waypoint. So it will look for **target1**, then, if the NPC is less than 1 meter away from this target, it will look for and walk towards **target2**, and so on.
- Once it reaches the last target, it will start to look for the first target again.
- This way, the NPC will go through a path that is determined by the target points.

So, that's the general principle behind it. As you can see, it's pretty simple, and the implementation will also be relatively straightforward. So let's get started:

- Open the **indoor** scene.
- Create a new Cube object (**Game Object | 3D Objects | Cube**).
- Rename this object **target1**.
- Select this object in the **Hierarchy**.
- In the **Inspector**, deactivate the component **Box Collider** for this object, by unchecking the component **Box Collider** (as described on the next figure). This is so that the NPC does not collide with this target. The target, here, is just to indicate the path to follow.

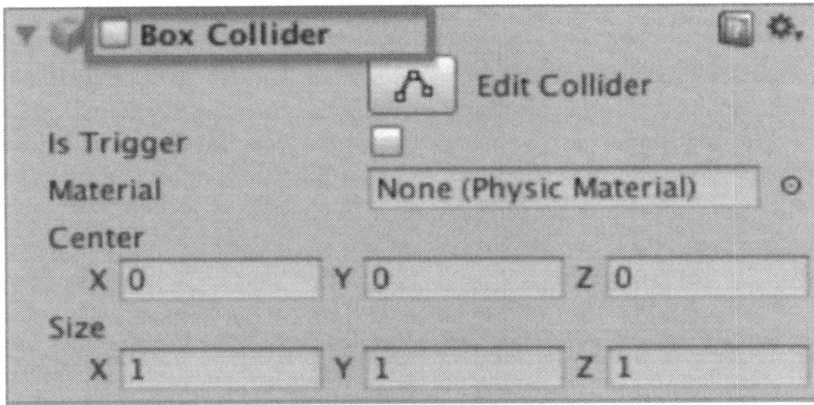

Figure 6-8: Deactivating collision for the target

- Check that the scale factor for this object is **(1, 1, 1)**.
- Also check that this cube is slightly above the ground.
- You can also, for clarity, add a red color to this object by either reusing a red **Material** that you have created earlier, or by creating a new **Material** and applying it to the cube (e.g., select **Create | Material** from the **Project** window).
- If you want this box not to be displayed later on, you can just deactivate its **Mesh Renderer** component also.
- Duplicate this object three times; this will create three objects labelled, by default, **target2**, **target3**, and **target4**.
- Place these four objects at different locations, creating a path of your choice; again, make sure that these objects are slightly above the ground. To focus the view on any of these objects, you can select one of these in the **Hierarchy** window and then press *SHIFT + F*.

Great. So we have just managed to define a path for our NPC; the next step will be to change the default script that is usually linked to the NPC, so that it follows the path we have defined.

- Select the object **target1** in the **Hierarchy**, and press *SHIFT + F*, so that the next object added to the scene (i.e., a new NPC) is placed near it (since the NPC will look for this target first).
- Add another NPC to the scene (this NPC will be using a path, while the first one will be following the player) using the prefab **AIThirdPersonController** located in the folder **Standard Assets | Characters | ThirsPersonCharacter | Prefabs**, and by dragging this prefab to the scene, near the object **target1**.
- This will create a new object labelled **AIThirdPersonController 1**.
- Rename this object **npc_path**.

- Select this object (i.e., **npc_path**) in the **Hierarchy** window.
- In the **Inspector** window, you will see that, by default, it will include a component called **AI CharacterControl**. This script basically tells the NPC to follow a particular target and is also used by the first NPC. In our case, we would like this NPC to behave slightly differently by following a path instead of following the player. So, we will modify this script so that the second NPC walks along the path we have defined.
- Double click on this script (**AICharacterControl**) to open it.
- As you open the script, you may notice that the syntax and structure of the file are a bit different from what we have seen so far. This is because it is written in C#; but not to worry, the next steps will be quite simple and all explained.
- Add the following line to the script (new code is highlighted in bold).

```
public class AICharacterControl : MonoBehaviour
{
       public NavMeshAgent agent { get; private set; } // the navmesh agent
required for the path finding
       public ThirdPersonCharacter character { get; private set; } // the
character we are controlling
       public Transform target; // target to aim for
         public int targetRank;//used to know what target to follow.
```

- This new line defines a variable **targetRank** of type **int** (integer) that will be used to determine the rank (or index) of the target to follow.
- Next, we will initialize the value of the variable **targetRank** to **1**; so that the first target is **target1**.
- Please modify the code (changes are highlighted in bold).

```
private void Start()
{
       // get the components on the object we need ( should not be null due to
require component so no need to check )
       agent = GetComponentInChildren<NavMeshAgent>();
       character = GetComponent<ThirdPersonCharacter>();
       agent.updateRotation = false;
       agent.updatePosition = true;
       targetRank = 1;
}
```

- Next, add the following lines of code (the code highlighted in bold) in the **Update** function:

```
private void Update()
{
        if (gameObject.name == "npc_path")
        {
                target = GameObject.Find("target"+targetRank).transform;
        if(Vector3.Distance(transform.position,target.transform.position) < 1.0)
        {
                targetRank ++;
                if (targetRank >4) targetRank=1;
                target = GameObject.Find("target"+targetRank).transform;
        }
        print ("Current Target is target"+targetRank);
}
```

In the previous code:

- We check whether the current object or NPC is the one that follows a path (i.e., name = **npc_path**).
- If this is the case, we look for the current target (e.g., **target1**).
- Then we check whether we are close to this target (i.e., less than one meter away), and if this the case, we increase the value of **targetRank**, so that we start looking for the next target (e.g., **target2**).
- In this case, we also check whether we have reached the last target (i.e., **target4**); and if this is true, then we go back to the start of the path by looking at and walking towards the first target.
- Finally, we print (in the **Console** window) the current index for our path (i.e., 1, 2, 3 or 4).

Eh voila!

Let's see if it works:

- Save your script.
- Switch to Unity.
- Play the scene and observe (using the **Scene** view, if necessary) how one NPC follows you, while the other one walks along a path.

If you encounter any problem, please check the following:

- The scene has been baked and all targets are slightly above the ground (e.g., less than 1 meter above the ground).
- The name of each target is spelt properly in the **Hierarchy** window.

- All targets are not too far away from the ground.

DETECTING COLLISION BETWEEN THE NPC AND THE PLAYER.

We have almost finished; the last elements we need to add is to check whether one of the NPCs collides with the player, and if this is the case, we can restart the current level.

- Open the **indoor** scene.
- Select the object **FPSController** in the **Hierarchy** window (i.e., the object for the player), and check, using the **Inspector** window, that its **tag** is **Player** (i.e., if this is not already done).
- Create a new script using the **Project** window (**Create | C# Script**).
- Rename this script **detectAICollision**.
- Drag and drop this script on top of each NPC in the hierarchy (i.e., **AIThirdPersonController** and **npc_path**).
- Add this code at the beginning of the class.

```
using UnityEngine.SceneManagement;
```

- Add the following function to the script.

```
void OnCollisionEnter (Collision hit)
{
        if (hit.collider.gameObject.tag == "Player")
        {
                print ("Reloading the scene");
                SceneManager.LoadScene (SceneManager.GetActiveScene ().name);
        }
}
```

- In the previous code, which will be linked to both NPCs, we check whether a collision occurs between the NPC and another object.
- If this is the case, we check for the tag of the object involved in the collision.
- If this is the player, then we print the message **“Reloading the scene”**, and then we reload the current scene.

Let’s see if this works:

- Save your script.
- Switch to Unity and play the scene.

- Check that it behaves as expected (i.e., scene reloaded when one of the NPC collides with the player).

Level Roundup

In this chapter, we have learned about adding and configuring NPCs to provide them with some levels of intelligence. We looked at simple behaviors (i.e., follow the player) and more advanced behaviors (i.e., following a path). We looked a little bit into C# code (hey!) to modify the default behaviors, and we managed to include more challenge for the player. So, again, we have made considerable progress.

Checklist

You can consider moving to the next stage if you can do the following:

- Add an NPC.
- Set a target for an NPC.
- Set a path based on 3-4 objects.

Quiz

It's time for our last quiz to check your knowledge. Good luck!

1. The function **onCollisionEnter** is called whenever a collision occurs between two objects with colliders.
2. After adding a target to an NPC, it should automatically look for this target (or is there another necessary step?).
3. Write the missing code to be able to detect the tag of the object colliding with the current object (linked to the script).

```
OnCollisionEnter (Collision hit)
{
	tagOfOtherObject = hit.collider.<MISSING CODE>
}
```

4. By default, an NPC with a given target will avoid all other objects (i.e., walk around them).
5. A waypoint is one of the reference points for a particular path.
6. Any scene can be duplicated using the shortcut *CTRL + D*.
7. The following code will reload the current scene.

```
SceneManager.LoadScene (SceneManager.GetActiveScene ().name);
```

8. What does this error message mean: **"; missing"**.

    a) You forgot to add a semi-colon at the end of a variable definition.
    b) You forgot to add a semi-colon at the end of a statement.
    c) All of the above.

9. What does this error message mean: **"unknown identifier"**.

    a) You forgot to declare the variable before using it.
    b) You may have misspelt the variable that you are trying to use.
    c) All of the above.

10. If the **Console** window shows errors and you can't seem to be able to play your scene, what can you do?

    a) Take note of the name of the script, the error message, and the column and line where the error was found.
    b) Fix the errors.
    c) All of the above.

Answers to the quiz

1. TRUE
2. FALSE (we need to bake the scene also)
3.

```
Void OnCollisionEnter (Collision hit)
{
        tagOfOtherObject = hit.collider.gameObject.tag;
}
```

4. FALSE (the scene needs to be baked)
5. TRUE
6. TRUE
7. TRUE
8. c
9. c
10. c

Challenge 1

Now that you have managed to complete this chapter and that you have improved your skills, let's put these to the test.

- Duplicate the **indoor** scene.
- Change the position of the targets defining the path.
- Play the scene.

Challenge 2

This challenge will be about adding a more complex path.

- Duplicate the **indoor** scene.
- Add three more targets (to obtain seven targets in total) and place them so that they form a path of your choice.
- Ensure that their name reflect their index (e.g., **target2**, **target3**, etc.).
- Modify the code of the script **AICharacterControl** so that it accounts for the fact that the path ends after the 7th target.
- Play the scene and check that it works.

Challenge 3

This challenge will be about creating a mini-map for the **indoor** level.

Please read through the section that explains how to create a mini-map for the outdoor scene and create a similar mini-map for the **indoor** scene so that:

- The position of the player is represented with a green dot on the map.
- The position of the NPCs is represented with a red dot on the map.
- The position of the items to collect is represented with a yellow dot on the map.

7
FREQUENTLY ASKED QUESTIONS

This chapter provides answers to the most frequently asked questions about the features that we have covered in this book. Please also note that some videos are also available on the companion site to help you with some of the concepts covered in this topic, including AI, UI, collision, cameras, or paths.

SCRIPTS

How do I create a script?

In the **Project** window, select: **Create | C# Script**.

How can I check that my script has no errors?

Open the **Console** window and any error should be displayed here.

What is the difference between gameObject and GameObject?

When you use the keyword **gameObject** in the script, it refers to the game object that is linked to this script. So **gameObject.transform.position.x** will refer to the x position of this object. However, **GameObject** refers to the class **GameObject**, from which you can access functions that you can use. For example, **GameObject.Find** gives you access to a function that you can use to find other objects.

What is the dot notation for?

The dot notation refers to **Object Oriented Programming**. Using dots, you can access properties and functions (or methods) related to a particular object. For example **gameObject.transform.position** gives you access to the **position** from the **transform** of the object linked to this script. It is often useful to read it backward; in this case, the dot can be interpreted as **"of"**. So in our case, **gameObject.transform.position** can be translated as "the position **of** the transform **of** the **gameObject**".

INTERACTION WITH ASSETS

How do I detect collisions?

To detect collisions from the **First-Person Controller** (player), you can use the function **OnControllerColliderHit**; however, to detect collision from another object, you can use the function **OnCollisionEnter**. In the first case, the script will be linked to (i.e., dragged and dropped on top of) the **FPSController**. In the second case, the script will be linked to (i.e., dragged and dropped on top of) the object.

How do I destroy objects?

To destroy an object, you can use the function **Destroy**. For example, **Destroy (gameObject)** will destroy the object **gameObject.** You can also add a delay so that the object is destroyed after a few seconds. For example, **Destroy (gameObject, 2)**, will destroy this object after two seconds.

How can I create a scoring system?

For a simple scoring system, you can create an integer and increase its value by one every time the player has collected an item.

USING A GRAPHICAL USER INTERFACE

How do I create a text to be displayed onscreen?

Select: **GameObject | UI | Text**.

How do I update a text to be displayed onscreen?

You need to find this object, and modify its text attribute. So to display the message **"Hello"** using a text object with the name **messageUI**, the following code could be used:

```
GameObject.Find("messageUI").GetComponent<Text>().text = "Hello";
```

How do I add an image onscreen?

Select: **GameObject | UI | RawImage**.

How can I empty (i.e., delete) the text onscreen?

You just need to set its **Text** attribute to an empty string; for example, the following code will empty the text field **messageUI**:

```
GameObject.Find("messageUI").GetComponent.<Text>().text = "";
```

How can I display the value of a specific variable onscreen?

You just need to access the **UI | Text** component where you need to display this variable and set its **Text** attribute, with additional text if need be; for example, the following code displays the text "**Score** =" followed by the value of the variable **score**:

```
int score = 20;
GameObject.Find("messageUI").GetComponent< Text>().text = "Score = "+score;
```

AUDIO

What is the difference between an AudioClip and an Audio Source?

Basically: The **AudioSource** is the sound system (or the MP3 player) that makes it possible to listen to a sound; the **Audio Clip** is the actual sound that you want to play.

How do I play a sound?

- Create an empty object.
- Add an **Audio Source** component to this object.
- Drag and drop the sound you want to play in the **Audio Source**'s attribute called **AudioClip**.

Artificial Intelligence

How can I add an NPC to the scene?

- Import the **Characters** Assets.
- Drag and drop the **AIThirdPersonController** prefab (from the **Characters** folder) to the scene.
- Set its target.
- Use the **Navigation** window to bake the scene.

How can I create a path for my NPC?

- Define waypoints.
- Add an NPC.
- Modify the script that controls the NPC so that it follows each target consecutively.

8
THANK YOU

I would like to thank you for completing this book; I trust that you are now comfortable with scripting in Unity and that you can create interactive 3D game environments. This book is the second in a series of four books on Unity, so it may be time to move on to the next book for the intermediate level where you will learn more advanced features, including coding in C#. You can find a description of this book on the official page **http://www.learntocreategames.com/books/**.

So that the book can be constantly improved, I would really appreciate your feedback and hear what you have to say. So, please leave me a helpful review on Amazon letting me know what you thought of the book and also send me an email (learntocreategames@gmail.com) with any suggestions you may have. I read and reply to every email.

Thanks so much!

Made in the USA
San Bernardino, CA
01 April 2018